Miner* Celebrity:

How an Underground Artist Found Fame in NYC.

By Marcus X. Taylor

**Not a typo, you dig…*

*Do you see a man skilled in his work? He will stand
before kings; He will not stand before obscure men.*
Proverbs 22:29; (NASB).

Table of Contents

Prologue (circa 2008)

The other night while walking in the Meatpacking District I saw Tracy Morgan driving down 9th Avenue in a yellow Lamborghini. So I yelled: "Tracy;" the way a person might yell at a celebrity, as if they actually know them. He kept driving only to get caught at the red light and that's when I decided to make my approach. So with the CD of my songs in hand, I made my way over to the vehicle, my hands in plain view, so as not to cause him any more undue alarm seeing that I was already violating his vehicle space. "Tracy," I offered: "Check out my record."

He accepted it and as I was highlighting its content and features I could see him starting to relax, even putting the CD down onto the passenger seat. So in light of him being at the light, I cut right to the chase: "It's for sale" I said and when the realization hit him that I was indeed trying to sell and not give my music to him- in one quick dismissive gesture he hands me back my CD, shrugs and says candidly: "I don't buy music." "I know," I replied trying to match his candor: "You buy Lambos."

Now the last time I ran into Tracy Morgan, he was at Big Nicks, the eatery on the Upper West Side, several years earlier. I had noticed he was driving a Jaguar back then, and was acting more like the Tracy Morgan you see on T.V. He was very animated, with a knack for storytelling that is unrivaled except for, maybe by Ice T. He dominated the conversation back then, and again he would dominate this conversation, mind you this all in the span of a traffic light. Now when I said: "I know you buy Lambos;" I was saying it in a congratulatory, I see you doing your thing- kind of way. However he took it as if I was saying: "Since you can buy that really expensive vehicle, you should give me some money." He must have that conversation a lot. He then told me something to the effect of, not to measure myself by what he has, and he also added: "I earned this." I say something to the effect of because by this point in our brief exchange I was momentarily confused. I tried to assure him that I was not measuring myself by his Lamborghini; when he continued: "I started out just like you; I used to be up in the Chicken Spot." Finally he said: "So you have a good night, alright Paw" (he must have thought I was from Brownsville), and so I simply said: "You too," and then he drove off.

The whole exchange though brief and ill-projected, was calm and contained. Tracy Morgan since I can remember, and in my opinion, has always been entertaining, so I can only imagine the hardships and headaches that go along with so-called "fame" at that level. There's a

Scripture in the Bible that reads: "For the love of money is a root of all sorts of injurious things, and by reaching out for this love some have been led astray from the faith and have stabbed themselves all over with many pains." That was true back then, and is still true today. Now as far as vehicles go, anyone who knows me knows that if I'm not walking in NYC, I'm riding in that M5, M8, or M14 Crosstown bus.

The Merchant of Greenwich

I talk to strangers for a living. I observe and study them looking for something, anything, to get them to stop and talk to me. In hopes of striking up a conversation and in turn-turn said conversation into a conversation about music. Then regardless of where the course of the conversation goes from there, my goal is always to steer subsequent conversation about music, to a conversation about my music. Sometimes it's just a matter of impressing these strangers with my limited, albeit above average knowledge of music. I say limited, because I really don't know that much about music- the same applies to film, literature, and art. As with many areas of learning the more you learn, the more you realize how much you really don't know. Knowledge is infinite and although my knowledge of music is narrow, it is nonetheless and often times wider than the majority of the people I have met. Once the conversation has shifted to music it is often just a matter of time before I am likely and finally asked about my music: "So what kind of music do you do?" Or: "How do you know so much about music?" The rest is, well, the rest is to be sold and not told. Regardless of the depth or lack thereof of my knowledge, I do know that anyone can teach me something, that I don't know.

People unlike knowledge are limited, especially in areas of learning; it is more often what we think we know about a given subject that limits us, more so than our actual knowledge or ignorance for that matter. When some of us know even a few minor details of a particular subject we tend to act as if we have it mastered, and can now file it away. Or like me are sometimes just content to be able to hold an intelligent though limited conversation on a wide range of subjects-this became all the more evident to me while talking to people about music.

Almost everyone you might assume you'd meet, especially in NYC, has heard of The Beatles, right? But how much do people really know about The Beatles? Are they able in the absence of any memorabilia, or at a glance at a stranger, to decipher whether or not he or she is either a fan of The Beatles, and or, The Rolling Stones; or in the rare case neither? Well neither can I, but what I can usually do is tell someone who considers themselves a hardcore fan something that they may have not known before, at least in the case of The Beatles.

I often find myself on the receiving end of these little tidbits, either through anecdotal exchange, or what at the time may seem like the accumulation of useless pieces of information, except of course, until it becomes useful, either while having a casual conversation or one with an intent to sale.

Whether or not we like to admit it, people think in types. Every day while pushing my music on the streets of NYC, and points in between, people would say to me before ever being told what kind of music I was offering: "I don't listen to Rap" or: "I don't listen to that type of music." Many of us are guilty of it- guilty by reason of vanity; because so much of what we conceive and believe is based on what we see and are accustomed to seeing. We use what a person may look like as an indicator, whether tacitly or overtly. Still we are guided by these purely topical observations however superficial we have found them to be in our past experience, and yet we persist- it is in our nature.

These kinds of pre-or-ill-conceived notions inform people's everyday thoughts, and reactions to other people. In the streets of New York City however one is reminded or taught that there are so many exceptions and few rules.

I talk to strangers- sometimes, the stranger- the better. In some ways I consider myself a social scientist. I make hypotheses, conduct experiments, and continue to test my methods in hopes of confirming my pre-supposed postulations, while simultaneously seeking to get my art of persuasion down to a science. I could tell you that I began this endeavor about 8 years ago, but that would not be the truth, in fact I often times try to retrace my steps, seeking to find the starting point, before the fog clouds my recollection and the precipitation of time covers those footprints in my mind.

Ah- it's all coming back to me now. Years ago, my cousin (by marriage, none-the-less a dear one) remarked to me one day while noticing the comparable size, smoothness, and resemblance of our hands, that we, him and I, were not meant for manual labor. He reasoned that due to our relatively small hands that we were meant to use the larger appendages, that of our brains for heavy lifting.

The fact that he and I also share the same birthday, no doubt, in his mind at least, added credence to his claim.

As I look at my now coarse hands, I can't help but wonder and hope whether or not he was right. I've been a dishwasher, lawn mower, pneumatic power tool assembler, doughnut packer (and not just in my mouth), cab driver, waiter, car salesman, and drug dealer (alleged).

I've shoveled snow, worked in the rain and the sleet, and had the oddest of the odd jobs. I've tried my hands at many exploits, some of which have led me to others and others that seemingly took me nowhere but I'm here- thanks to God.

Much of these happenstances occur in or around the Village in New York City, on 6th Avenue to be precise. When I was first introduced to the "Hustle" as we call it, I stood alongside a group of guys who names were and are: Creature, Shake-O-Blaize, Sensational, Big D, Sub Con, AB Do Well, and a guy ironically enough, called Unknown. Before I got to the block, there was already a legacy that had begun spawned by the likes of Percee P, Lifelong, and Jin the MC.

Now we were your regulars who stood outside of Fat Beats, a now defunct independent record store that was located upstairs at 406 6th Avenue near 8th Street, in what some would call the West Village. A native New Yorker however might argue that there is no distinction, that there is just, "The Village," or rather Greenwich Village.

Our office as we called it was outside downstairs right in front of the record store. We would beckon customers as they entered and left the record store and other passerby alike. We were not the only guys in town though. You had similar crews (Infinite Marvelous, Timbo King), on 42nd Street in Time Square outside of MTV, and the Virgin Mega Store that was located there, and the surrounding areas. You had the 14th St. Union Square crew; Jerms Black, Hill, Bones Don, and J Freds, and also a couple of young ladies, Nina B, and Nemesis who worked the Virgin Mega Store that was once located at one time there in Union Square during the day.

I also worked outside the 14th street, Virgin Mega-store, but at night.

You also had the Duo Live crew out on Broadway near where Tower Records used to be located. Wherever there was a major record store, there was probably someone setting up shop outside.

We'd go on "tour" as we called it, which meant that we'd usually stroll from 6th Avenue down to Broadway on 8th Street and then either head north towards 14th Street or south down to SoHo.

We would see the other hustlers in our travels and exchange pleasantries, admonitions, and sarcasms.

H the Great was another guy who hustled both day and during the night as well, and who also became an author some time ago himself.

Most of the other hustlers would at some point call it a night, but I would more often than not, work until 1:00 AM; when the Virgin Mega-store usually closed, and then see where the night would take me, the destination usually- to trouble.

The police for the most part would not bother us. Every so often someone would complain about being harassed by us which, more likely meant being annoyed and the cops on a couple of occasions showed up and gave us a good talking to, which is to say yelled.

They were especially hard on the guys that worked 42nd Street though. Being that tourism specifically concentrated in that area is such a life-line to the city, I figure they were just protecting their investment.

"This, That & 23rd"

You also had guys like, Mes Ones, Kosha Dillz, J-Bully, 360, and Sav Killz, interesting monikers I know, but with the personalities to match.

On our (my) first walk up Broadway together towards 23rd Street, I remember it like it was yesterday, the guys discussing amongst themselves, but loudly if I was indeed, "ready" or not? Of course I felt I was, but unlike 6th Avenue down in the Village, where people would walk either north or south and occasionally from across the street to pass by or enter one of the several stores that lined the block. On 23rd Street people came and went in all directions, and because of the subway station situated right underneath where we stood, people even came from underneath the street. I learned to really think on my feet, and to carry on multiple conversations while beckoning on comers as well.

In the car business when someone would come through the door we would what we called "qualify" them. In other words ascertain whether or not they were indeed good prospective customers. We would do it through a series of pointed questions; work history, credit history, and marital status. You could do this over the course of the interview while getting a better feel for the customer (guest).

On 23rd Street, we had only seconds. Of course the stakes weren't as high as selling a car, but the job was the same- to make a sale.

It is a natural reaction for a person to feel either rejected or intrigued by the waning interest of the salesperson in front of them, especially when the interest has shifted to another prospective customer.

The ole offer, and retract offer dynamic is a tricky one.

However when attempting to sell a high ticket item such as a car I would not advise this, because the guest could very well make you regret it by either buying a different car, or worse- buying the same car, but from a different salesperson.

With music on the other hand, and especially so-called underground music, it was easy to create an illusion of a greater demand through the frenzied nature of our approach to the business-yelling, talking fast, loud and exuding confidence. Sometimes it would work as a catalyst and at other times, not so much.

I especially enjoyed the scenery of 23rd Street, the Flatiron Building standing right there in front of us, and Madison Square Park off to the right.

Whereas in the Village there were a noticeable amount of artistic types, on 23rd Street there were all types and a substantial corporate presence as well. I learned that our approach not only appealed to artists who often championed us, but also it was appreciated often times by business people, lawyers, investors, and financier- types who applauded our entrepreneurial spirit and industriousness.

I had so many interesting exchanges with so many interesting people. I once befriended a woman named Tina who, as it turned out managed the Blues great BB King. As a result I was able to take my mother to see him perform in Poughkeepsie, New York, and during his show he passed out little gold necklaces, and my mom, being right up front, was one of the proud recipients. She also made a Banana pudding to give to him via his manager. I don't know what ever became of the dessert, but it was a nice thought, my mother making a Banana pudding for BB King.

Seth Green walked through 23rd Street, and picked up a record from me one afternoon. He was both gracious and generous. Chloe Sevigny also picked up record one day, and afterwards went and sat in a nearby café and had lunch by herself.

I continued to work while glancing through the window, gauging her progress, and when she was almost done eating I sent her a chocolate cake for dessert. I thought it was a nice touch. However when I ran into her again years later, this time around 1st Avenue, she seemed to have little recollection of it all. I understood though having met so many people myself. It is impossible to remember everyone both the sweet, and thankfully the bitter.

I had read some place that Chloe used to baby sit for Kim Gordon, and Thurston Moore of Sonic Youth. I would meet Thurston Moore sometime after meeting Chloe, and instead of asking him about Chloe, I asked him what he was currently listening to. He responded with some obscure black metal band, but then added that he was reading a book that he really enjoyed by a guy named John Joseph, from a band called the Cro-Mags. I mentioned that I knew John (Creature had introduced us years earlier), and that I would relay his appreciation to John, which I did.

This, during the time when Creature and I had a residency at the Knitting Factory when it was located on Leonard Street in Tribeca, before it moved to Brooklyn. A guy named Peter Agoston who was a talent buyer there, hooked us up with the residency. Peter had heard of our work ethic, and so provided what would be the backdrop for what proved to be one of the most memorable periods of my artistic growth.

Thurston Moore and Lee Renaldo, both of Sonic Youth had played that night at a special event for one of the major guitar companies. There was no Steve Shelley or Kim Gordon in sight, however on another night while I was standing all alone on 6th Avenue, which was unusually silent, and empty for that time of the night, being only about 10 or 11pm. I saw this silhouette of a woman, then blond hair, and then I could make out her face, it was Kim Gordon, walking in my direction from several yards away. I stopped her, and told her that I was a fan and about having recently met Thurston Moore some time back. I also mentioned to her that I had recently picked up a copy of *Daydream Nation*, Enigma, 1988; one of their bands' most critically acclaimed albums.

I told her that I was a big Pearl Jam fan and had read some place that Eddie Vedder had hung out with her and her family at one time. I kind of took her by surprise as I jumped all over the place. She seemed a bit bewildered but she kindly picked up a record anyway.

I would later meet Steve Shelley while hustling outside a small record store in Chicago. I was in Chicago, interestingly enough for the Pearl Jam Twenty festival that the band threw in celebration of their twentieth year anniversary. It would be held in Alpine Valley, located in East Troy, Wisconsin, and as the date approached I had no idea how I would get there; I only knew I had to go. Part of the reason the band chose Alpine Valley, we were told, was because of its proximity to 3 major cities: Chicago, Milwaukee, and Detroit.

I chose to fly into Chicago because my homeboy Luke was attending Columbia College there. Luke, at the time, happened to be the current resident DJ for my Fire Your Boss presents event that I had resumed at the Bowery Poetry Club.

I asked Luke if I could crash at his place, and he said yes, but he informed me that he had roommates (Katie, Skyler, and Andrew) who all welcomed me both with open arms and beers, plus they were foodies to boot.

So I flew into Chicago, but still with no definite ride to the concert in Wisconsin. So I placed an ad on Craigslist offering a ticket to the show, in exchange for a ride to and from the festival.

I advertised that the seats were "good" although I knew I would have to pick them up from "will call;" being that they were from the band in all.

Stone Gossard one of the guitarist and founding members of Pearl Jam had hooked me up once again, so I assumed that as usual the seats would be great.

After a few nibbles I finally got a bite, a girl who wanted to discuss some of the finer details over the phone. Once we were on the phone I could sense her reservation which after we hung up turned into her

E-mailing me that she was no longer going to the festival, which I found hard to believe for a Jammer (as fans of Pearl Jam are called). Just when I had all but given up hope on getting to the concert another girl named Keela contacted me. We arranged a phone call and right away I could sense the apprehension in her voice as well. What followed was one of the most candid conversations I have ever had with a complete stranger. She told me basically that although she wanted to help me out that she was afraid, because, as she put it, she was: "Just a little white girl from Indiana."

I told her that I completely understood having experienced I suspected, a similar sentiment, although unstated.

You see I know I don't fit the usual profile of a Pearl Jam fan - which is to say I'm black. The prospect of coming to pick up a complete stranger, a guy none-the-less, and a black guy in Chicago was probably too much for the other girl to wrap her head around.

I can't really blame her though. For no other reason than when it comes to certain situations, a woman, of any color, can't afford to be wrong.

Once I put Keela at ease, she agreed, no I should say, she resoundingly resolved to come back and get me. She had already driven an hour passed Chicago on her way to Wisconsin, and if she hadn't come back for me I don't know how or if I would have made it to the concert.

We got to the venue, which is a huge outside amphitheater, just as the The Strokes were finishing up their set.

I had just saw Nikolai Fraiture, the bassist for The Strokes days before, in New York, while standing in front of the Blue Note Jazz Club on West 3rd Street.

I asked him what he was still doing in New York when he was supposed to be in Wisconsin. I half-jokingly asked if I could catch a ride with them (the band), except I wasn't half joking.

I told him that I would see him out there, and that I didn't know how just yet, but that I would.

Now as Keela, and I, and one of her buddies (whose name escapes me) who we met up with at the venue made our way to the backstage area for refreshments, The Strokes were just coming off the stage.

I called out to Nikolai as he was walking from the stage and told him: "I told you I would see you out here." He smiled, came over said hello and shook my hand and then disappeared behind the stage with the rest of the bands I imagine.

I had met Fabrizzio Moretti the drummer for the Strokes before meeting Nikolai, this when he and Drew Barrymore was an item. They both showed me love, and picked up my record in Union Square.

Glen Hansard (The Frames) also took the stage that night; this was before _Once_ the film directed by John Carney, Samson Films, 2007; that he starred in, based on the life of a busker in Ireland, opened as a Broadway musical.

I had met Glen on 6th Avenue a year or two before the festival. He also picked up a record as we discussed some of my other favorite bands from Ireland.

I asked him about Bell X1, and The Republic of Loose, the latter having performed at one of my Fire Your Boss shows during our stint at the Knitting Factory.

I just recently saw a piece that was done on Glen on CBS, and immediately understood why he had been so down to earth, and cool, because that's how he is. Even now, back home in Ireland the street musicians still respect him- he's still a busker at heart.

Dennis Rodman was also in the backstage area, but it seemed like he didn't want to be bothered, but since it was Dennis Rodman, and since he's black, and I'm black, I figured I'd go over and give him the obligatory secret handshake, and he obliged. Needless to say the concert and whole experience was amazing.

Being on 23rd Street taught me that you didn't need a storefront in which to stand in front of, ultimately like I had learned in the car business, you're selling yourself after all, but not in a derogatory sense. Everything I needed was God given, already stored inside, and all I needed was to prepare for what lay ahead- in store.

Sheryl Crow walked by one afternoon heading south on Broadway. I'm a fan of Sheryl's, and as inopportunity would have it, she was on the phone, but I was still able to get her attention, and get my album to her as she apologetically signaled that she couldn't talk. I wanted to tell her how a bunch of us black guys used to listen to her while lifting weights in an unlikeliest of places, a camp called, "Wyoming."

Sometimes though, people use their devices as a means of deflection. I actually watched people purposely pick up their phones as they would approach one or more of us, in an attempt to avoid having to engage or be engaged by us. But like the song says "I was married to the game" So it wouldn't be that easy to deter me. I had to tell one guy that he was holding his phone upside down, and so it was obvious that he wasn't having an actual conversation.

One of the most difficult obstacles I faced in putting myself out there, so-to-speak, was actually having the resolve to do it. As artists, I think we sometimes tend to have a romanticized vision of how success should and will unfold for us. That someone will automatically recognize our talent, hard work, share our vision, and become our benefactor. That may be the exception, but the rule is, most venture capitalists, venues, and companies, no matter what the nature of their business, won't do business with any artist unless that artist has generated some interest beforehand. I got wind of that fact early on in the eve of the turn of the century. When I first got to NYC, back then all me and my aspiring colleagues did was run from one record company to another, thinking that motion was the same thing as progress.

I started to realize even back then, that if you had the where-with-all to gets an actual buzz going, It may behoove you to do as much as you could on your own, and then if necessary, or the opportunity presents itself, partner up with a company; the operative word being partner, each bringing something to the proverbial table, because if you're not bringing something to the table then you're probably just taking something off of it.

More and more you hear horror stories of artists who have sold in some cases, millions and millions of albums only to have to file for bankruptcy. I don't mean to over-simplify the matter either. I realize that there's not one avenue that is always bad, and one that is always good. That's just it though, there is always another avenue. I found mine in New York City, and in the open- air markets- all demographics are afoot.

Living in NYC, if not much else, will teach anyone willing to learn, how to plot a course to a destination, and to do it with the most ease and convenience, circumventing interruptions of service and re-routes along the way.

The culture of materialism and reckless spending that is so pervasive, especially in Hip-Hop, and that is fostered by the record companies in some cases, only adds to the high incidence of artists falling into destitution.

An associate of mine Ben who does contract administration in the music business; and has done that kind of work since about the time I got wise to the game, advises that artists should only take a big enough advance to get the project done, and pay a few bills if they have to.

Instead of spending money on expensive items like jewelry and cars which are more geared towards celebration than work. I have seen it also with my own eyes. An artist gets signed and then it's a big party, but that's when the real work begins.

I've been in numerous studios and heard often times mind blowing music, but it's the work that one is willing to continue to put forth that counts. That's maybe part of the reason why I prefer the blue collar approach. Of course I want to make money but I also want it to be understood that any money, if there is any, was and is made through hard work. So many artists continue to fake it even after they have made it, but you can't even fake hard work without putting forth effort.

One day Amy Poehler walks by while I was standing on 6th Avenue. I had long admired her skits on NBC's *SNL*, and maybe in my mind I imagined that in person she would be like one of the characters she portrays on the show. The "One Legged Cheerleader" perhaps. Now granted I'm a bigger than average black guy and even the average black guy is bigger than the average white woman or women in general.

I offered her my record and she shied away, almost squeamishly from me. I felt some kind of way. I mean it was broad daylight and I had bathed and was clad in clean clothes. At first I was really offended and put off because my thinking was: "She imitates, at times, albeit in comedic fashion, the manner in which, at least in her comedic sensibilities, some black people speak, so how dare she be timid."

Now I didn't expect that she would be Miss Black People, or that she'd give me five on the back hand side (okay maybe I did), but I didn't expect that she'd react in the manner in which she did, especially since I had encountered so many other actresses, and comedians, even from NBC's *SNL*, that even if they didn't buy a record, were not as apprehensive as she seemed. I mean I couldn't get Keri Russell to stop for nothing, but at least she smiled at me once, after about 2 years. After some time I understood though, regardless of how I may see Amy, I'm still a stranger in her eyes.

One night not too long after that, at almost the very same place, Bill Hader also from *SNL* happens by in a group, with at least one of the writers from *SNL*. So I called out to him, and when he seemed reticent, I told him not to: "Go getting all Amy Poehler on me."

I would also complain somewhat- to the same effect, to Seth Meyers at a later juncture- again in almost the same spot there on 6th Avenue. What I didn't realize, and should've in those failed attempt to endear myself to them, is that they're all like family, close family at that.

Bill Hader in an interview with Charlie Rose on PBS even credited Amy Poehler with helping him during a crucial moment during his audition process for *SNL*.

Now tell me, who has ever thought about being famous, and has not thought about being on *SNL*? However If I have burned any bridges along the way, and I'm sure that I have, then one must understand that those bridges, just happened to be there, suspended over those ships that I burnt in the harbor.

Several years back when my show, *Fire Your Boss* was gaining a lot of momentum, as a new show in NYC often does.

I couldn't accommodate all the prospective performers and artists who were interested in performing. However this one guy kept hounding me about being on the show and as you could imagine megalomania started to set in. Despite his keen interest instead of reaching back out to him I blew him off relishing probably in that moment-being sought after.

Looking back now at how I treated him, I know my behavior was rude, nonsensical and counterproductive- just a short while later those were the kind of artists I clamored for.

One day I got a message from that same persistent artist who had reached out to me to no avail. He berated me, right from the gate and he berated my show as well. He told me that he didn't need my, "little show," and that he was going to do even bigger and better shows.

As I was reading his literal literary tirade, I felt a shift in my perspective. I was no longer upset at what I was reading. I felt inspired, because although it hadn't been my intention, I helped him to free himself of relying on, or reaching out to me. He realized I imagined, that he didn't want or need his success to hinge on someone who didn't even have the courtesy to open the proverbial and literal door for him- I wish him well to this day.

So many artists today, especially in the mainstream seeing that they're more visible, remain inaudible about speaking out on injustices that may be considered controversial for fear of hurting themselves in the pocket. You'd be hard-pressed to find a bad review about an influential artist or company, from a popular source, because so many are beholden to them. You have this, this symbiosis of stardom via media and vice versa- where the writer and the subject depend on one another to continue doing what-it-is, that they do.

Big corporations understand that any artist is expendable, especially when you have a big check book and a plethora of would-be-whatever-you-want-them-to-be artists, waiting in the wings for their chance to take flight.

I realize now that an adversary can motivate you as much as an ally can, sometimes even more, because you're not deluded by the possibility of being lent a helping hand from an adversary, if and when the need arises, because you know where you stand.

That being said I'm still a fan of Amy, Bill, and Seth's; though I am still intent on running my own little show. Plus now I'm not as surprised, or disappointed when people are not who they pretend to be.

On another evening, as I stood, as it was also my habit, in front of Electric Lady Studios, where Jimi Hendrix once called home right there on 8th Street, not far from 6th Avenue. The door to the studio swings opens and out comes Aaron Neville. My first reaction was, wow, and then as I made my approach I smiled and nodded as I told him what a big fan I was and still remain of his. As is also my habit, I went on to say something that I felt like kicking myself for, later that night during my nightly review of the day's events. Instead of broaching the subject of his music, I remarked to Mr. Neville about something I had read in Bob Dylan's book Chronicles, Simon & Schuster, 2004.

As I was trying to recount to him the bit about Bono suggesting to Bob Dylan that he ought to go down to New Orleans and search out the Neville Brothers, I thought I imagined hearing a woman's voice saying: "Marv." Seconds later as I continued to grapple for the recollection- still face to face with Mr. Neville, I again hear: "Marv." Finally I turned just to my left where the voice was coming from, and it's this woman, Sarah, who I had initially met when she was going out with this guy Beans from the group, Anti-Pop Consortium.

I reply, somewhat startled by the abrupt distraction: "Sarah;" still trying to process her face. She replied: "Yes" and then introduces Aaron as her husband to me.

It was obvious my confusion amused her as she went on to explain to Aaron that I was a friend of Beans, and before she could continue,

I quickly interrupted her to clarify that I was more- friendlier with Beans, than friends. I added that I was not trying to disown him in any way, but that he was tight with Creature, and when Creature and I dissolved our business relationship a few years back, it was like Beans was one of the associates/assets Creature kept in the dissolution.

Sarah then asked me how Creature was doing. I told her he was blessed and that I had seen him not too long before then, after having not seen him for some time. I mentioned to her that Creature had even become a father recently.

I then handed Mr. Neville my album, not having the gall to ask for the sale. I told him about my show, Fire Your Boss, and as I do all artists I admire, regardless of status- I invited him to come perform.

I asked him about his schedule, and he replied as I might have expected that he wasn't exactly sure of his itinerary.

I figured that the worse him, or any artist could say to my proposition to perform, is no, which would render the same result if I hadn't asked in the first place. If I don't ask then it's automatically no, If I do ask- I only stand to gain. Even if the answer is no, at least the conversation has been started, and who knows, maybe- just maybe?

I have nothing to lose except what I hadn't possessed in the first place, it's a win, and if not, when?

I assume, based on the timing of events, Aaron was then finishing up his Doo Wop project that he put out with noted music producer and president of Blue Note Records, Don Was and also Keith Richards.

Don had picked up my album on 6th Avenue a year or so before and was super cool as he walked down the Avenue, flanked by none other than John Mayer.

It had been some years even before then, that I had first met John Mayer while hustling outside the Virgin Mega-store that used to be on 14th Street.

I saw him through the plate glass window one evening as he was about to check out at the cash register. I was already in position right outside in front so as to catch people coming in and out of the store.

I had a good vantage point of even being able to see when people were in line at the register, and whether or not they paid with cash which is also important.

A female emcee by the name of Nemesis who I hustled alongside with, once or twice, told me of her shoe test. Each time a person engaged her she would glance down at their shoes, especially in the cases where the person appeared to be a bit riff-raffish. You could have a person whose dress left something to be desired, but whose shoes told a whole different story. I'm not sure why it worked; was the condition of the shoe indicative of how much the person walked, which correlated or spoke to a necessity on their part? Are shoes a vain and guilty pleasure and thereby informative of disposable income? Was it just a matter of class- on all different levels? Had she at one time worked in shoe sales, and it was one of the many, and varied axioms you find true in every line of work, but specific to that particular industry? I don't know either way, but I've since become more and more intrigued by the idiosyncratic.

When John Mayer came out, I handed him my record with the admonition: "Check it out" and he asked me right away if it was: "Any good?"

I replied without missing a beat: "I am invincible." He countered with: "Yeah but is it any good?" I then repeated: "I am invincible" and then I added: "As long as I'm alive." He finally realized that I was quoting back to him his own lyrics from his song "No Such Thing," from his album *Room For Squares*, Aware/ Columbia, 2001. He took the record but didn't pay me that night, however it was John that insisted on buying the record the night when Don Was, was reaching for his money, on the aforementioned occasion.

Electric Lady Studios has been the back and front drop of many of my so-called celebrity run-ins, especially due to it being just around the corner from 6th Avenue and where I once stood.

There were so many points of interest there in that short stretch of the 600 block of 6th Avenue : Gray's Papaya, the Bagel Buffet, upstairs from the Bagel Buffet, you had Fat Beats, next door to Fat Beats you had and still have Life Thyme, a very popular health food store and restaurant and favorite of many familiar faces. You also have Bigelow's, the drug store adjacent to the corner of 9th Street which also caters to a number of film and television personalities beside common folk. I got my music to David Alan Grier there, and also Kelly Coffield near there as well, she as you may remember, starred alongside David on Fox's *In Living Color*.

Jeffrey Dean Morgan of ABC's *Grey's Anatomy* walked through, the gauntlet; that's when there's a bunch of us nestled together hustling in two rows facing one another, a sort of Soul Train Line for sales. He was very generous and picked up a bunch of music. Oh and I can't forget about Sandra Oh, she came through the block, and got a record as well, but not through the gauntlet.

I spoke briefly to Jane Krakowski on one occasion, and even though she didn't get a record she was nice enough, in fact I didn't even offer it to her, it just wasn't the right time or place.

T-Bone Burnett another well-known music producer picked up a record from me as he walked south on 6th Avenue one afternoon.

I told him that I loved his work and that he and I had a mutual friend in Adam Duritz of the Counting Crows. T-Bone has produced some of my favorite records from Adam and many others.

I also told him that if he just agreed to walk into the studio as I worked, and turn the lights on and then off, in the room, that I would give him production credit on my album. I didn't' say it to seem like I would be doing him a favor and so I hope it came off as homage.

I imagine he wouldn't want his name anywhere attached to any production unless he actually produced it.

The same day I saw T-Bone, I also saw a semi-familiar looking older gentlemen. He was well dressed with a cardigan type sweater draped around his shoulder, arms twisted in the front. He looked like either a director or an international playboy, which in some cases are one in the same. As he walked passed I said, as I extended my hand, CD at the ready: "I'm a director myself." He smiled, walked right up to me, and extended his hand in introduction: "Hi I'm Joel Schumacher." I remembered right away that among his other titles that he had directed were <u>Batman Forever</u> & <u>Batman & Robin</u>, Polygram Filmed Entertainment, 1995, and Warner Bros, 1997 respectively, based on the DC Comics character. I had also read that he had taken some harsh criticism for his vision on the franchise.

As I was grappling for another title to his credit, he chimed in with: "D.C. Cab," RKO Pictures, 1983, and "<u>Car Wash</u>" which was written by him, but directed by Michael Schultz, Universal Pictures, 1976. He picked up both my albums as I went on to mention to him that Michael Keaton had patronized me as well, some years before.

As you might remember, and as did I, midway through naming some of my favorite films of his, to Mr. Keaton; he was the original big screen <u>Batman</u>, directed by Tim Burton, Warner Bros, 1989. At least the first one I ever saw on the big screen, and with much regale. He assured me that indeed he was, but in more colorful words.

Out of the few titles I mentioned to him in my conversation with Mr. Keaton were: <u>One Good Cop</u> (dir. Heywood Gould, Buena Vista Pictures 1991), <u>Beetlejuice</u> (dir. Tim Burton, Warner Bros, 1988), which I never actually watched; and <u>Johnny Dangerously</u> (dir. Amy Heckerling, 20th Century Fox, 1984). I neglected to include <u>Jackie Brown</u> directed by Quentin Tarantino, Miramax, 1997, based on the Elmore Leonard novel <u>Rum Punch</u>, Harper Torch 2002. The film was a favorite of mine. I recall the scene where he's rubbing his chin in contemplation and his motorcycle jacket squeaks; just that one moment said a lot without any dialog-it's the small things I tell you.

While growing up, and before I would have ever given any serious thought to moving to New York. I would watch movies and shows filmed and set in NYC, and just the sight of the ubiquitous yellow cab excited me. I imagined re-enacting some of my favorite scenes and dialogs from my many favorite films made here.

Even now if I'm crossing the street and a cab veers too close I still say, "We're making a movie here." In homage to Dustin's Hoffman's alternate line in <u>Midnight Cowboy</u> directed by John Schelsinger, United Artist, 1969, written by Waldo Salt, and based on the novel of the same name by James Leo Herlihy, Simon & Schuster, 1965.

On another occasion the actress Lynn Whitfield, in response to me asking her to check out my record, responded with: "I wish I could sell my own movies like this on the street." Now I don't know if Ms. Whitfield was being genuine or not, she is after all a gifted actor, but I would offer that she could very well sell her own films on the street if she so desired or needed. Or maybe she was just trying to placate me, you know like the quote from Al Pacino's Michael Corleone in the film directed by Francis Ford Coppola, Paramount Pictures, 1974, <u>The Godfather II:</u> "Discontent for money is just a trick of the rich, to keep the poor without it;" which was partially based on the novel <u>The Godfather</u> written by Mario Puzo, G.P. Putnam's Sons, 1969. I would also offer to Lynn or any other artist that you can make a living selling yourself, without selling out.

Chuck D asked me when I first approached him with my record, after he had performed in Washington Square Park alongside Deborah Harry of Blondie one afternoon: "Am I going to hear you saying something?" Meaning was I talking about something on the album, or talking about nothing? That questions still stays with me even up until now.

I watched one night as India Arie related to Tavis Smiley, as she sat with him on his program on PBS that, and I'm paraphrasing, she at one time would judge artists based on their musical content.

However after she had been misjudged for something herself, she was reminded that any artist or any person for that matter can move on and forward from any moment creative or otherwise. In other words the snapshot is not the whole picture of the person.

I found that to be so profound, not only because of what was said, but who said it, and what is more, who she said it to.

You see I had met Tavis myself in front of the Blue Note Jazz Club only months before. I asked him about the director of his show Jonathan X, and he was appreciative and impressed enough to buy my record- no questions asked.

I knew though from watching his show that Tavis is a religious man, and that particular album he bought from me, doesn't reflect my values, or his I would imagine. It's a dark album, recorded during a dark period of my life, compounded by the fact that it is missing some crucial songs that I wanted to add to kind of round off the overall theme of the record; instead the record that I ended up putting out ends on a very negative note.

What's even more interesting is that when I first hit the Avenue to start hustling my music, there were some people who we red-flagged. That is to say, we avoided even approaching them. Be it an unstable person, which was more frequent than not, seeing that hidden in between those famous stores and points of interest, near where we stood on 6th Avenue, were some psychiatrists offices as well.

India Arie was on the red flagged list not because she was unstable or psychotic, but because she had garnered a reputation on the block for not buying records. I presumed in part because of what she thought our music might represent.

So I judged her for thinking she was judging me. So when she would come and leave out of the health food store, most times I'd just keep silent.

Conversely she went on to perform a song that night on Tavis that she wrote called "Break the Shell," from the album Songversation, Motown Records, 2013; that she said was inspired by Cicely Tyson, and by the time the episode aired I myself had also met Ms. Cicely Tyson, at of all places, the Blue Note.

Ms. Tyson was there with, Kimberly Elise, (who actually looks like a younger version of her), Angela Bassett, and her husband Courtney B. Vance. I offered my record to Angela, but she respectfully declined. I told her it didn't matter though, that I was still a big fan either way. Just as they all hopped in a town car and were pulling off, I realized that Courtney B. Vance had starred in one of my all-time favorite films, The Last Supper, directed by Stacy Title, Sony Pictures Releasing, 1995; alongside; Bill Paxton, Ron Perlman, Cameron Diaz, and Nora Dunn et al.

They must have thought I was a mad man as I ran to flag down the town car as they rode away; maybe that's why they kept it moving.

Around the same time I had run into Ron Perlman again, he had already picked up my record previously, and we had talked about that same film, this before all this Sons of Anarchy business, I told him how much I had enjoyed the plot and the performances, so I just kept it to a fist bump. Anyhow, I said all that to say that I had judged India Arie because I assumed that she was judging me.

Jesus commanded that his true followers: "Stop judging...;" It's a constant struggle to not be judgmental, but I have since stopped using profanity, and obscenities in my music, and in general, so Mr. Smiley: "Check out my new record."

On another occasion while I was standing again in front of the Blue Note, I saw Michael Moore getting into a car. I quickly approached, said hello, and mentioned to him that I had sat not far from him at a Pearl Jam concert at Madison Square Garden a while back. He was gracious and picked up a record.

That particular concert was a special one for me. It was my first complimentary show at The Garden, compliments of the band at that. I took this Dominican kid Jonny who I was unofficially mentoring the first night, and I took my then 12 year old son with me the second night which really rocked. After the first night I was able to introduce Jonny to Stone Gossard who had arranged the tickets for us.

Both nights rocked, but the first night was subdued in comparison to the second. On the way home my son remarked that his ears were ringing. It had been so long personally since my ears had rung after a show that I felt somewhat guilty, knowing the ringing meant that he had suffered some damage to the cells in his ear.

I told him however that when the subject of first concerts arises, and it will. He'd have a good one to tell. I hope that the memory for him lasts longer than the ringing did. Jonny if I might add, has become somewhat of a guitar-prodigy.

Danny Masterson, and Ben Foster, who is one of my favorite emerging actors, was also at that same show.

Ben was cool; I spoke with him for a bit about an interview I had seen him do on Conan, back when he was doing Late Night on NBC.

On that particular show Ben was promoting his film <u>Hostage</u> directed by Florent-Emilio Siri, Miramax Films, 2005; Co-starring Bruce Willis and Kevin Pollack. It was a lively interview and a good show all around, from the guests, to the musical guest that night- the late great Solomon Burke.

I have yet to meet either Kevin or Bruce.

Kevin however was in the film, <u>The Usual Suspects</u> directed by Bryan Singer, Gramercy Pictures, 1995. Gabriel Byrne, who was also in that film was a regular sight on 6th Avenue, and picked up my record himself some time ago.

I remember at the time being so tempted to say one of his famous lines from one of his many films when I saw him coming down 6th Avenue. I considered maybe, <u>The Usual Suspects</u> written by Christopher McQuarrie or <u>Miller's Crossing</u> directed by Joel Coen; 20th Century Fox, 1990; but memory failed me on the latter, and as for the former I thought it inappropriate to blurt out: "There's no coke" in the middle of 6th avenue in broad daylight, or in any light for that matter.

I also offered Kevin Spacey my record, one night, but he declined although he seemed to enjoy my little "check out my record" routine that I was performing in front of the Blue Note as he stood there smoking a cigarette and taking in the sights, and sounds of the evening.

I encountered Sigourney Weaver one evening as she walked hurriedly toward the door of the Blue Note. The show had already started and as I offered her my record she explained that she was late, and that she had no money on her right then. She seemed so sincere, and since I'm such a fan of her body of work as I explained to her, I just told her to take it. She assured me that when she came back out she would pay me, but I wasn't sweating it, she had the record already.

I quickly added that I had recently watched <u>Heartbreakers</u> directed by David Mirkin, MGM 2001, for the first time, on television, and enjoyed it.

True to her word after the show she came out, and made a bee-line towards me. She handed me some cash, and I was thankful, and somewhat taken a back at the thought that she sat through the whole show with the thought of paying me, "the guy outside", before she left. That's why I tell people, the reason why opportunity has to knock is, because it's outside.

With few exceptions I rarely asked for pictures and if ever for autographs from famous people.

I guess I wanted to keep these seemingly unbelievable moments unbelievable.

It reminds me of the scene in <u>Forrest Gump</u> directed by Robert Zemeckis, and written by Eric Roth, Paramount Pictures 1994; where Tom Hanks, as Gump is relating all these fantastical stories to a group of captivated and bemused folks at the bus stop. After all but one, a lone older woman, leave; Gump then offers to show the woman what: "Lieutenant Dan looks like;" this after the gentleman who had just departed remarked how tall the storyteller's tales were. You really note the woman's surprise and additional wonderment at the related accounts as she comes to the realization, after being shown Gump on the cover of Fortune magazine, standing beside Lieutenant Dan, played by Gary Sinise, that he had not been making it all up after all.

Likewise, I myself have to be somewhat oblivious to people's doubts. You have to be really, in order to accomplish almost anything.

I think it was Einstein who said something to the effect that unless an idea seems completely absurd when it is initially introduced, it has no hope of succeeding.

So I caution would be skeptics to both; not be so skeptical that you end up missing the best part; and I don't just mean the bus, and also that they may want to keep a look out for me on the cover of Fortune magazine.

At the time of this writing I have not met anyone that I recognize from the movie *Forrest Gump*, but I still have some pages to go.

So it is with an admitted absurdity that I soldier on with these accounts. It would be a waste; a waste not to tell how being at the right place (space) - at the right time, has led to explosions on all different levels. The gravity of which I have probably yet to fully appreciate; how sound, light, and vibration, in more than one case, precipitated the actual physical manifestations, of terrestrial beings held in almost celestial lights. Some who've shone brighter and larger than others, all who courses through the cosmos brought them within my magnetic field of perception, but what does it really matter, except only in an effort to put Einstein's theory of Relativity in a social setting.

Yes I know it sounds over the top, and astronomical, but that's New York isn't it, where ideas are as big as the buildings.

Now there's a thought, what if in fact, the size of a city's thinkers is commensurate to the size of its buildings? To think I wasn't even on any of their radars. Which goes to show that just because someone isn't on your radar, doesn't mean they're not in flight.

"Catch Phrases"

You've no doubt heard the expression "catchphrase" I would imagine? Well in my line of work, some phrases were in fact just that. Designed and delivered in a way so as to catch people's attention. Most sales pitches like most songs engender hooks.

People in NYC for the most part are so desensitized when it comes to beckoning strangers, that catching and what is more holding people's attention is quite a feat. Once you add getting them to dig into their pockets, well then you have what I like to call a formidable challenge.

One of my own and a very personal favorite catchphrase of mine goes: "You must be an actor?" Sometimes I would deliver it in a whimsical tone or in the face or should I say, the back of rejection, I would make it sound like more of an indictment.

The punch-line was always the same: "Because you're acting like you don't know who I am and you're being very convincing."

I can't tell you how many actors, aspiring actors, and regular folk, who may have fancied themselves as actors, I was able to "catch" with that particular line. When you actually consider it though, that is what most of us are-actors.

We despite our innate tendency to conform, like to believe, (if we believe at all) that we perform these acts of conformity in our own unique ways, and we're right to an extent. We play many different roles and often times the same role in different ways.

The world is full of clichés that speak to the "two types" of people. Each cliché is fraught with universally unique, yet at the same time unifying differences. Usually the person offering the "types" does so from the position of the more advantageous type- the doer. Most people like to think they make some kind of difference. People also like to think that what they do they do like no other, which may be true but to a smaller extent than most would like to admit.

The reason being is there are too many people and too few recognized things to do so uniquely that you stand alone. Wise King Solomon was inspired to write that there was "Nothing new under the sun;" this was true even during his time- processes and cycles.

No matter what one's perceived level of success is or isn't, people appreciate doers. Sometimes it's as hard to imagine someone else doing what you do, as it is imagining another actor playing the part in one of your favorite films, in place of the actor whose portrayal you have come to love, and have grown accustomed to.

However actors pass on roles all the time and in many cases weren't even the directors or studio's first choice- some to their chagrin while others-grin.

While out there pushing our music on the streets of NYC, and points in between, and doing so unabashedly and unapologetically we attracted people. There was magnetism to what we did.

People were drawn to our counter-culture-anti-music-business-establishment resistance of the status quo.

They rooted for us, maybe because deep down inside they stopped rooting for themselves. Dreams and aspirations become burdensome especially when life starts to bear down on you.

People cave; and I mean that in the sense of giving in, and also in the sense of hibernating in a creative sense. Being preoccupied with the bare necessities, and putting something away for a cold or rainy day.

Simply surviving seeking and storing sustenance, waiting out the thaw, going out mainly for the, not necessarily needed things, which sometimes amounts to just getting fat, season after season, teaching our offspring to do the same.

What is this fascination with celebrity all about? It seems to be more about recognition than hard work. An individual can work their butts off for years, with little or no recognition. While others find it, and then find themselves in the company of people, some with whom they would have ordinarily had little or no access to.

People with new found stardom are welcomed into the bunch as if the welcoming committee, consisting of the already famous, were on the sidelines egging on the nascent.

Take for instance someone like Gabourey Sidibe, made famous by her starring role in the movie _Precious_ directed by Lee Daniels, Lionsgate 2009, based on the novel Push by Sapphire, Knopf, 1996. Gabourey, although a relatively new star, is probably more recognizable than say an

Austin Pendleton or Wallace Shawn, the latter two having both been in over one hundred productions, and both patrons of mine.

Wallace Shawn bought my record in front of the IFC Center, and Austin Pendleton in front of the Blue Note, and night after night he would walk pass me, and we'd nod at each other as he'd stroll down the street unaccosted.

I spoke with Gabourey one night outside of Greenhouse a nightclub in SoHo, as Scram Jones was spinning records inside, and although few people approached her, it was obvious that people knew who she was. I told her that night how much I had enjoyed a segment she and Wendy Williams (a whole other story altogether) had enacted on Wendy's show on television, (Debmar-Mercury, 2008).

Maybe the difference is that Gabourey was the central character in the previously mentioned film, and as it stands, I think we gravitate to the center, not noticing or hearing necessarily or as loudly, the people in our peripheral.

Work ethic aside, people want to be recognized and reckoned alongside the recognizable, even famous people themselves.

Rubbing shoulders with the newly inaugurated famous sometimes, as if hoping that the spores of fame continue to spread, and are tracked from one budding career to another, sometimes even re-germinating the ones that have begun to wither, all under the radiant and quasi-illuminating light of fame.

A catchphrase that worked even before I hit 6th Avenue to hustle, and especially with famous people was: "It's me;" Shake-O-Blaize, and Creature were very adept at wielding this particular set of words. So I quickly made it a part of my repertoire, in fact everyone who stood outside where we stood did, and I must say it worked.

I came to understand after some time, the dilemma that famous people especially sometimes face. Being that they meet so many people, they can't possibly remember them all, and due to the nature of their business, and often times, their own good-nature, they don't want to offend anyone, especially someone that they probably should've remembered.

After a while they usually caught on to my facetious farce, but by then they were hopefully somewhat relieved, amused, and a customer.

I had a funny exchange with Mo Rocca outside in front of the now departed Barnes & Noble store once located on the corner of 6th Avenue and 8th Street, which was one of my "satellite offices".

I told him it was: "Me," and as he studied me searching my face for any trace of familiarity or fraud, I kept on assuring him that it was indeed: "Me". Journalist, whether they're famous or not, especially like to be in the know, but after a short while I just wished him well and he walked off.

Even before I started pushing my music independently on the streets of New York, I was never one for autographs; it just never did anything for me. As a kid I used to collect coins, and even now I find it hard to throw anything away that I think may one day be of value. However a name on a piece of paper is just that to me, unless someone is endorsing a check I could care less about having their signature.

Kathy Bates (who I have yet to meet and who I only spotted once from inside a moving bus) related an experience she had, to one of the late night talk show hosts about an autograph seeker.

This person had approached her very enthusiastically for an autograph as she was walked her dog in the Village in NYC. She complied only to find upon rounding the corner some minutes later, and needing paper to pick up after her pooch, that very same paper she had autographed now laying on the ground. So as any self-respecting dog walker would, she used it to scoop the poop, which I found funny and indicative of the fleeting nature of our culture's fascination with the famous, and of the inherent evanescence of fame ever more evident in this, instantaneous albeit, disposable information age that we live in. It's hard to keep many people excited about much, and for long.

There's a dichotomy even apparent in the use of technology. People like many features, and high output, but in relatively small devices on one hand, but when it comes to their viewing pleasure, a demand for the largest screens available still exist. We want our dreams and fantasies to remain big.

In the car business we would "spot" vehicles, meaning we would let the prospective buyer take it home for a day or two, even for the weekend. Knowing that once a driver has driven, and what is more, been seen driving a new vehicle, it's all the more difficult to return the vehicle, yes, we like our shine, even if we can't afford it.

That is why people pay big money to go to the movies, and even bigger money for concessions because it's part of the movie going experience. Think about it, would you pay seven bucks for a small bag of rice? That's pretty much what a bag of popcorn amounts to.

When my son was about 4 or 5 years old we were on our way to the movies, and so I made a quick stop at a bodega, and picked up some snacks. Once we were inside the theater, I dug into my bag during the previews and produced a big bag of cheddar cheese popcorn, but my son would have none of it, you see in his mind the popcorn at the counter was superior to the popcorn from the bodega.

It wasn't a matter of taste, or freshness- only his perception.

Sometime actors themselves are more recognized for their features, than for their features. Probably one of my most effective catchphrases was: "My music is like poetry- at the speed of sound." People often said they liked the way that it sounded, that it had a nice ring to it. I would tell them truthfully, that it was part mine, and part Paul McCartney's.

***

Before the inception of my *Fire Your Boss presents…* event, I tried my hand at promoting a Beatles Party. First at a place we called Charmains down on West Broadway that has since disappeared like so many other establishments. Then at a cigar-bar called Circa Tabac, down on Watts Street and finally at Karma, a Hookah bar on 1st Avenue, between 3rd and 4th Streets.

The week before the "Paul is not Dead" party we threw at Karma, I had met Steve-O, from the Johnny Knoxville, Spike Jonze and Jeff Tremaine created, for MTV, *Jackass*, at the Pyramid club. He and his lawyer, a guy named Jason had dropped in to check out the open mic. Steve-O even got up onstage to talk to the crowd a bit, and show off his new tattoo of himself.

After he came offstage I invited him and his people to come to my upcoming "Beatles" party at Karma, which was just an Avenue away, and low and behold they showed up.

Having a Beatles party was the brainchild of myself and a guy named Richie (we're gonna need a bigger book), who is from Utica as well; although I first met him while he was living in Harlem.

Richie gave me a crash course on almost everything The Beatles put out, as a group, and individually.

His favorite Beatle is Paul so a lot of the music we listened to, centered on Paul's solo stuff with his band *Wings* and even one of his alter-egos "The Fireman".

I never knew that Paul had recorded so many songs and with so many people or even about his artwork.

I even named my website at the time Paymrcleancut, which is an anagram for Paul McCartney- I still use the email to this day.

Richie put me up on a lot of music that I didn't know about and even music that I once thought I knew.

When I first started hustling music outside of Fat Beats I met Sean Lennon and talked with him briefly about listening to The Beatles after only re-discovering them in my 30's.

I didn't tell him about how Richie, myself, and this guy Mark "The Hooker Driver" (don't ask) went down to Howard Stern's show when Paul was scheduled to appear, and waited outside for the Beatle.

As Paul's car pulled up Richie and I made the "Wings" symbol with our hand, which come to think of it, bears a resemblance to the WU- TANG Clan's symbol. Members of the WU who now refer to Scram Jones as the Scrza, because of all the work he has done with Raekwon, and Ghostface, over the years, but I digress.

Paul was at that time in company with, and married to Heather Mills, and when he saw Richie and I making the "Wings" sign we could see him tapping her and directing her attention towards us, and then he summoned the driver to stop, and Sir Paul McCartney hopped right out of the car and stood between Richie and I.

I was speechless as he told the group of waiting admirers and autograph seekers that he could only sign a few.

When I looked at Richie he looked mortified, but in a good way, if that makes any sense.

His facial expression was one of part disbelief, and part wailing, but tears of joy- only minus the tears.

Richie kept repeating in whining tones, like a terrible two-year old nagging a parent: "I know you're going sign mines Paul;" only he was cursing in intervals, not maliciously or even with an obscene intent.

It was utter disbelief, and a torturous skepticism that the moment was too good to be true, and that Paul would disappear at any moment.

I was working as a waiter at that time, and was still in my uniform from the night before. I can now appreciate more, what Richie was feeling. Paul was like a genie in a bottle that he had been rubbing on for so long.

***

One day Anne Heche bought my record; now as a rule I don't share what, if anything, people have paid me for my music, but I told Anne, and she agreed, that whatever she paid me would be the equivalent of $500, so Anne Heche bought my album for $500.

Usually when people question me about numbers I like to be more abstract than specific, when people ask me how many CDs I moved in the streets, I tell them truthfully, not enough, but more than they might think.

Later that evening this kid named Los came by Fat Beats, and after we spoke for a minute, he asked me if I was going to the Raekwon show at SOB's.

I knew Los from my days in Poughkeepsie, and I laugh sometimes, to myself when I say the name of that city, because I recall the scene in the film, State of Grace, directed by Phil Joanou, and written by Dennis McIntyre, Orion Pictures 1990; where Sean Penn's character asked John Turturro's character contemptuously: "Where you from, Poughkeepsie?"

John Turturro picked up an album from me as well. He also attended SUNY New Paltz, which is just over the bridge and not too far from, ta da, Poughkeepsie.

I had thought that the Raekwon show was on the 15th, but that was the KRS-One, and Buckshot show. KRS-One had told me that himself as I stood onstage with him and members of BDP, and Scott La Rock's daughter, after the tribute they held for Scott at Irving Plaza, two weeks prior.

I asked Los if he had an extra ticket, or a plus one and he shook his head, sheepishly grinning which I took to mean that he did but not for me.

I figured I'd call Scram since he had worked with Raekwon on the album for which the release show was for that night, and as I reached for my phone, I saw I had a text message from this kid Kadi, who managed Kurious Jorge.

I had just featured Kurious on one of my Fire Your Boss presents shows, this one at a place called the Annex that was located on Orchard St. The message from Kadi read: "Any family wanna roll to the show tonight gotta get in with us, the show is sold out."

I texted Kadi back, and arranged to meet up with him in front of SOBs to get in the show, and I did.

The place was packed, and as Scram took the stage to set up, chants of WU-TANG, WU-TANG, went up, followed by chants of Rae-Kwon, and I could tell the crowd was getting antsy.

As a promoter I've learned the fine line between building anticipation, and or aggravation.

As we waited for the show to start, I thought back to the time when I had first met Raekwon.

Russell Simmons had put on a mini fashion show for MTV. I was at that time still relatively new to New York City, and as you might expect, I was trying to attend every industry event possible.

A guy named Beef who I had been referred to by a guy named Chuck, who I had spit (an inner city colloquialism meaning "recited") a verse for in Joe's Pub, and who was impressed enough to put me in touch with Beef, had begun mentoring and managing me at the time.

Beef would remark about how all the 30k a year millionaires would always be out in full force at those kinds of events, trying to look the part hoping to get the part.

Maybe he was trying to tell me something back then me with my velour suits and shades.

Oh and chewing gum, because everyone knew that every successful rapper needed bubble-gum.

While we were all in the green room at MTV, and as I tried to seem unimpressed and very accustomed to being in those surroundings, I finally mustered up the courage to ask Raekwon if I could spit something for him. His reaction was something you might expect from someone who you asked to borrow money from. His response was: "Awe, man, nah I got a headache."

I laugh about it now, but at that moment I was crushed. It must've shown on my face because immediately thereafter he said: "Nah son go ahead and bust your gun"; but the damage to my ego had been done, and everybody knows that a rapper with a damaged ego is not a shell, but merely a husk of himself.

So I told him: "No, that's alright," and then walked away, my tail between my velour covered legs.

I smiled and clapped as I watched Raekwon take the stage that night, backed by Scram on the turntables at SOB's.

It was rare, and endearing to see a rapper of his stature so genuinely appreciative of the good reception that his album had received. I guess when you've been at both the bottom and the top; sometimes you're content to never reach either extreme again.

He announced from the stage that at that time, his album *Built 4 Cuban Linx... Pt II*, Ice H2O/EMI Records, was beating out Jay Z's *The Blue Print 3*, Roc Nation, Atlantic, on I-tunes, both titles, were follow ups to what are considered classics albums from both artists.

Lyfe Jennings showed up, and Wyclef also hit the stage to show love.

I didn't attempt to speak with Raekwon that night, nor ever really after that, even having been in the studio with him and Scram once or twice over the years. Not since the great MTV disappointment of Two thousand and something.

Not that I harbored any resentment towards him, in fact the opposite is true. I just didn't want to step into his limelight.

Sometimes an artist or any eager individual can come on like strong cologne that just needs to boil down a bit.

Also by that time I had met so many other people who I respected, and admired, and so I wasn't as impetuous.

Hey if you stood in any artsy affluent neighborhood in New York City, in the same spot for hours with the express purpose of meeting as many people as you could, you would find in those thousands of "ordinary people," clusters of famous people as well. Wise King Solomon the most famous and richest person of his time said under inspiration that the accumulation of wealth and riches was like, "Chasing after the wind."

Tao of Two Cities

A little over what is now 13 years ago, my comrade Fortunato Crook and I ventured down to a club called 205 on Chrystie Street on the Lower East Side; 205 was actually the number of the address. I was new to the City, and Crook was just visiting from Utica, New York.

Crook and I grew up in Utica, and we both prided ourselves on being, among other things, dope emcees.

They held an open-mic that night, and part of the reason why I went there was to meet this dude, Scram Jones. My cousin Mustafa had told me about Scram. He also told me to get in touch with another kid name Wicz when I touched down in New York.

So I did, and met up with Wicz in front of the ASCAP building one afternoon.

Wicz as it turned out, along with a couple of guys named Chaoz and IZ, worked with Mustafa on some music back in Ithaca. Scram was at the same time attending Ithaca College and even had a popular local radio show called the "Chop Shop," with Eric "Daytabase," Lee as his radio station manager and fellow DJ.

They all knew each other from Ithaca, and we, my cousin, Crook, and I all knew one another from back home in Utica, which is funny because especially in NYC, the city that people most confuse Utica with, when I tell them where I'm from, is Ithaca.

I even asked a couple of people from Ithaca if it's the reverse and they affirmed that it was.

I must say that Fortunato and I both rocked-we did our thing on the microphone that night.

Crook especially impressed me with how he stood out- A Utican amongst New Yorkers, shining.

Individuals, in one way or another connected to these two cities, Utica and Ithaca would help spawn movements that would reach deep into the New York underground, and even around the globe, because let's face it, in New York, local is global.

Scram however, wasn't the DJ that night at Club 205, which was more of a bar than a club.

The bartender told me in fact that Scram would be launching a new event the following Sunday on Orchard Street, not far from where we were, Orchard & Stanton, and the place was called Baby Jupiter.

So the next Sunday I made my way down to Orchard Street on the Lower East Side to meet Scram, and it was there that the End of the Weak open mike was being held.

It is now one of the longest running open-mikes in New York City, and by extension, I would think, the world.

Some renowned and celebrated emcees and producers have graced their stages; Immortal Technique, Jin the Emcee of 106 and Park Freestyle Fridays fame, Scram Jones himself a triple threat; Emcee, Producer, and DJ, plus a plethora of lyrical wordsmiths, musicians, and producers.

It was also where I honed my skills, and it has since spanned across the globe, and fostered other shows and performances like the Fire Your Boss presents event. That was first held at the Bowery Poetry Club, and then represented at the Knitting Factory, the Annex, The Netherlands, and even at the now re-established home of the EOW, the Pyramid club on Avenue A and 6th Street in Manhattan's East Village. Every success story has a point where somebody meets somebody at someplace.

Fast forward 10 or so years later, one night I get a call from Scram, and he tells me that he's got this DJ gig downtown on, would you believe it, Chrystie Street. Not far from the bar where I initially went to meet him.

I should tell you that the name Scram Jones is a jail colloquialism. I don't know if it started there, but that's where I came to know of it. Scram is a non-descript way of addressing someone in a contemptible way. When you don't want to dignify someone with a name you'd say "Scram," and depending on the level of contempt you may even leave off the Jones part.

That's not to be confused with the guy that's tipping out with your wife or girl, his name, like the song says, is "Jody".

So I knew even before I met Scram that I would like him just from his choice of moniker. I myself lean towards the self-deprecating, and comical.

Anyways Scram tells me that the gig he's got is some kind of Burlesque show. He said it wasn't nude, but rather tasteful, and that he'd be providing the music in between shows.

He also said that Alexandra Richards would do the opening set. So I made my way down to the club, and once at the door I was given a once and then twice over by the bouncer, and then a pat down, and I was in.

Scram and Alexandra's table was right by the DJ booth. They had bottles and chasers on deck as well. I mean I was accustomed to your cranberry and orange juice chasers, but this place (The Box), had fresh squeezed watermelon. I just drank the watermelon juice alone after a while, feeling somewhat self-conscious about asking for more watermelon juice, for fear of not embodying any stereotypes, but I'll have you know, that white people like watermelon just as much as black people do, and also, for those who partake, fried chicken.

After her set, Alexandra then joins us at the table with some her of girlfriends, a set of twins, and another guy and girl.

I didn't really take notice of the dude, but the girls were all gorgeous, cool, and free-spirited. Alexandra and I spoke a bit about music, and I asked her what she was currently listening to. She rattled off a few names, and then added, in the interest of full disclosure, and the obvious, that of course she listened to The Stones (her father being Keith Richards).

The night was moving along nicely and as it progressed in walks Sean Penn.

Now Sean Penn is one of my favorite actors, but he is also reputed to not be the most affable guy at times. So what did I say to him? Did I mention any of his legendary roles, or his humanitarian efforts in Haiti, and during Katrina?

Nope the first thing that pops into my head about Sean Penn is that he's good friends with Eddie Vedder so being fresh back from the PJ20 festival in Wisconsin, I tapped him as he walked by, but he just kept walking. Like beautiful women, I imagine stars get prodded in clubs all the time.

Later that night and when he walked passed again; I tugged on his coat, and said: "We have a mutual friend, Eddie Vedder." He responded: "Eddie is not my friend, he's my brother." Then I began to excitedly tell him about being at the festival, I was gesturing and talking very animatedly, so much so that when I sat back down at the table one of the twins asked: "So what were you arguing with Sean Penn About?"

I told her it wasn't an argument and immediately felt stupid for not commending him on all his humanitarianism. I actually expected to see Sean Penn at PJ20, I didn't expect to run into him at a club, especially since I'm not really the club type.

I also expected to see Tim Robbins at the festival, but I would see Tim within weeks of my return as well. He was riding a bike up Second Avenue. My son and I were heading to Porto Rico on Second Avenue to see the barrister for a cup of coffee. I yelled out: "Tim" at the top of my lungs, and then a second time.

My son and I were still a half a block away from him, but he stopped, probably not even knowing who I was, as we hurried in his direction. I said hello and introduced my son to him, and remarked that it had been awhile. I told him that I was surprised not to see him at PJ20. He asked me how it was, and I told him it was awesome. I then sensed that he may have been a bit perturbed at me for yelling his name like a maniac. Come to think of it, I wouldn't even have yelled like that for my best friend, it definitely required some delusion on my part.

I had initially met Tim when he was walking up 6th Ave with a hockey stick. Now he's a towering figure besides, but when you add a hockey stick, not many would tread at all, and if so, lightly. Tim ended up supporting multiple musical projects of mine.

There was even a point that I would see him and we'd chat for a bit out on the Avenue, and then he'd be off. Once he called out to me as he walked by, because for some reason I hadn't noticed him passing by. He's a big music fan, and a musician in his own right, and besides Pearl Jam, we talked about some Punk bands as well. His longtime partner Susan Sarandon just picked up my record more recently. I mentioned to her that I had heard one of their sons was a DJ. I also mentioned that I produce my own show at the Bowery Poetry Club and was always looking for talent.

I had met a young director some months later. Nicholas Jarecki was his name. He had directed Susan Sarandon in his film Arbitrage, Lionsgate, 2012, also starring among others, Richard Gere. I dropped Susan's name to him, and mentioned that I had watched his interview on Charlie Rose on PBS. He was gracious and supported me as well.

I had actually run into Ms. Sarandon years back even before running into Tim. We were at Irving Plaza for Pearl Jam's secret show. As she came out the side door somebody in proximity to me, I think made a rude remark to her. Till this day I don't know what was said, I only heard laughter, and seen her double back to give the whole group of us a glare, and the peace sign.

I didn't even re-visit that incident with her, things were going rather nicely, plus my boy Jay, a rapper who happened to be from Staten Island, and rubbed shoulders a lot, gave me some good advice once.

He told me that because in New York people are so accessible, when you meet famous people that you've may have met before. Unless it was a really good previous meeting, and a jarring of their memory would yield good results, it's better to let sleeping dogs lie, so-to-speak. They may even remember you over the course of the conversation, or night. However if you press the issue, still with no recollection you ruin the elusive and rare second chance to make a first impression.

I remember telling someone that I wanted to write my name on the proverbial bathroom wall, in regards music and the arts, but that was a fatalistic view. The statues people build in honor of other people, end up being mainly for the birds.

Richard Gere flatly refused my record on the corner of Broadway & 8th Street, but in a Zen kind of way. Him being a Buddhist, and the whole forsaking of worldly possessions in all, I relented, but If you ask me if I ever sold a record to a Buddhist, even one in full raiment, my response would be: "Does the Dalai Lama like syrup on his pancakes?"

Bowery Poetry Club

Although I had heard rumors and rumblings of the Bowery Poetry Club, being sold, I was still taken by surprise by the abrupt unfolding of events as I perceived them.

After having a stellar year there, and preparing to hold my own little music and film festival.

I got an email, to the effect that my next show would be my last. All of us who were privileged to have a show at the Bowery Poetry Club should be happy and proud. One thing that New York has taught me especially about venues is that legendary venues are made legendary not by the bricks and mortar, but by the flesh and blood that has graced them.

At the BPC, I not only had the opportunity to perform alongside some of my favorite artists, I had a hand in booking them.

Camp Lo was in February of 2012, R.A. the RUGGED MAN, was in March. Grand Daddy I.U., Cormega, and newcomer Nitty Scott MC followed. The year before was Homeboy Sandman in November.

Finally to round it off Large Professor's album release in July.

If you would have told me back in the early 90's that I would not only share, but also provide a stage for the Large Professor to perform on, it would have seemed like wishful thinking, thank you Gustavo Guerra.

Creature and Shake-O-Blaize both ended up hosting their own events at the Bowery Poetry Club also.

I welcomed the idea of putting my own stamp down, especially on a club in the Bowery, right there in the shadow of CBGB.

Before the closing of the BPC, rumors again swirled about its re-opening.

So for months I would walk by to see what, if any revamping was going on.

The fall and winter came, and still nothing. I took sick and had to be hospitalized, for a bit and re-located, but during my periodic visits to the City, still nothing.

One day after I had re-settled back in area, I walked by and saw the door open, and heard sounds emitting from inside. As I approached the now unfamiliar door and stepped in, I looked at where the tables used to be, and now there were different tables, the kind that require a coaster.

To my right, where at one time there was a café that served sandwiches, popcorn, cookies and drip coffee that Volcom had at one time occupied- and- it was no more. There was now a full bar, and not your dive bar kind of bar either, replaced by the kind of bar where Knob Creek Manhattans are served -straight up.

The bar-keep, a well- dressed man who, because of him looking me over, combined with the now ultra-sophisticated décor prompted me to ask his permission to see the place.

Mind you this was a place where I had recently had free reign. Now I was being told that I was not allowed to go passed the hostess podium.

It wasn't the same place where every second Thursday of the month, in recent history, Marvalous & Friends would present Fire Your Boss.

I had not too long shook hands with Lou Reed and Richard Belzer in this place. They along with Paul Shaffer had been there to check out a show called "Poor Baby Bree," a vaudeville styled puppet show, which preceded my show for a time.

I asked Paul Shaffer to give my regards to Tom Leopold. Tom is a comedy writer among other things. He had written for Seinfeld, and was friends with Paul Shaffer. I knew that because, Tom had bought my record right after I watched him and Paul go their separate ways one afternoon on 6th Avenue.

There was no more, Duv, a fellow artist and staff at the Bowery Poetry Club, and there was no love. No more tuna fish sandwiches, now it was Tuna Tartar.

I remember telling myself that if I ever met Lou Reed, I would ask him why he just didn't say: "And all the black girls go…" Instead of all the "Color girls go…?" on his song "Walk on The Wild Side" RCA 1972. Looking at him though, I just didn't have the nerve to; plus I'm not sure if the song is about girls anyways.

One day a kid named Chaz Kangas who supported many of us in front of Fat Beats, and is an emcee, and artist himself, called me and said that Donald Glover aka Childish Gambino, needed a last minute venue to perform at, this on the eve of my night at the BPC. I said yes of course, and have never seen the Bowery Poetry Club fill up so fast, and the show was one for the record books.

Here's a copy of an email I got from filmmaker Debra Granik years ago after she picked up my record

marvalous-

I bought your street beats the other day on 6th Ave. I'm the woman who has the movie at the Quad cinema. Did you check it out yet? If you can get there and get some friends there two good things can happen.

#1 the distributor will believe that the films we make, though small, are worth it. #2 this means that I can make a film with interesting artists such as yourself and they might take us seriously cuz we showed that people will show up.

Here's the information: QUAD cinema on W.13th street between 5/6

Avenues. 1, 3:25, 5:45, 7:50, 10. Hope to see you there.

Sad to say I didn't go to see Debra's film, for whatever reason I just didn't go, and I love movies. Maybe I was caught up with something or someone that day. Either way I should have heeded her appeal, because she was calling for solidarity. For a while I regretted not going. In turn she has never responded to or accepted any of the invitations for my shows as well. We as independent artists need to stick together. Not allow ourselves to be pitted against one another in any arena. In the underground Hip-Hop scene in NYC, there is this guardedness when it comes to audience especially. Many artists try to hold off on inviting their core audiences to some shows, while seeking to garner new fans from other artists' shows. Hip Hop isn't dead; it's just down on its knees like chivalry-get it?

If only a handful of people came to my shows (sometimes only a handful did) then they were unique visitors, probably never having been to my show. You must consider though, I was meeting new people every day. This before Analytics and Crowd sourcing really came to the fore. Artists like us out in the streets asking for "reasonable donations," and accumulating contact information, were the original kick-starters and for that matter, we were something like TMZ but in a smaller zone, even before TMZ but more along the lines of celebrity sightings than gossip.

The pay us what you think is fair model, was even adopted by Radiohead in 2007 when they self-released their album *In Rainbows*. Trent Reznor would follow suit for his album *Ghost I-IV*.

Of course I wasn't the only one who was patronized by movies-stars, athletes, celebrities chefs, the Intelligentsia, and others of acclaim.

My wide range of interest, and keen eyes just made me more adept at recognizing, and even sometimes sensing that the person who stood before me, or was approaching was renowned for whatever it was that they did. Julian Schnabel for example- just had artist written all over him.

That little film that I was invited to by Debra Granik was called _Down to the Bone_ It starred among others Vera Farmiga, who I adore. Debra has done pretty well for herself, since then. She followed up with a film called, _Winter's Bone_, Roadside Attractions, 2010; starring Jennifer Lawrence who has since become an Oscar award winning actor, and who like Vera Farmiga, besides being very talented, is also very easy on the eye.

Do I stay up nights and wonder what could've have been? Well I do stay up nights, but what I wonder about is what to do next, as I'm sure everyone does when contemplating and crafting their next project.

***

As I was standing where I stood, one afternoon, there on 6th Avenue, downstairs from Fat Beats, and in front of the Bagel Buffet's plate glass window; a town car pulls up, and out hops Mickey Rourke.

He saunters pass me into the café, and kind of took me by surprise.

Usually I can see people as they approach, and when I do see someone, and if I get really excited like I often do, I have a moment or two to compose myself, and gather my thoughts.

I was late extending my arm to offer him my music as he had already walked passed me through the door, just as I was just getting the words out.

He did acknowledge me though and told me to give him a minute. I gave him his space not following him inside, because I didn't want to crowd him.

What I hadn't supposed, and should have suspected was that others would notice him. This was right during all the raucous surrounding The Wrestler, Wild Bunch, 2008, the film by Darren Aronofsky that was being touted as his come-back film. He was as they say in Hollywood, hot again, and so as people began to swarm around him, he quickly darted back to the town car shoving a few crumpled bills in my direction, but without taking the music.

I felt somewhat defeated as I had gone over in my head in the few brief moments while he was inside, what I would like to talk to him about.

However In what would seem like a span of a few years, this time in front of the Blue Note I noticed a tricked-out black van coming down West 3rd Street, the kind of van that the S.W.A.T team might use.

That section of the neighborhood always has a very high police presence, so I assumed it was one of the many vans that come by prior to the blue and white police vans that can be seen hauling loads of the accused away. My heart goes out to some of those individuals when I see them all packed up in the back of those vans.

Guilty or innocent, Central Booking, one of the places where the police take you for processing, is no place to be. Men lying on the floor and all over the place, dope fiends, "dope sick" and throwing up, with one solitary exposed toilet, incomplete with no stall or cover, thrown in for bad measure.

I paid close attention as the tinted out van rode by. The window on the passenger side was down, and as the van rolled passed me I could see that it was Mickey Rourke in the passenger seat-I thought: "I got him." The light changed at almost that exact moment and so the van stood idle backed behind a few vehicles and ended up almost flush to where I was standing. I walked right up to the passenger side, grinning from ear to ear, and handed him my album. I told him that I was out here promoting my album, and it wasn't for free.

He told me that he didn't have his wallet on him because he was headed to the gym. He even asked the driver for confirmation, which he gave. Which I thought was so cool, because he owed me nothing.

Plus he wasn't in any way intimidated by me, he just felt my pain. I told him that he could have the record, and that I was a fan, and then I added: "Plus you were cool with Pac." He replied to my reference to the slain artist, that: "If Pac was still alive, none of these rappers could even hold his jock-strap." I so appreciated the old-school parlance and thought it very apropos, because I could imagine Tupac saying the same thing. I didn't even recall until afterwards that he had already thrown me a couple of dollars some years before.

Either way it was a priceless moment.

I also mentioned to him that I enjoyed the movie The Wrestler as he pulled off.

Marissa Tomei is also in that aforementioned film alongside Mickey Rourke. I saw her come by the Avenue one night, and as I tried to solicit a response from her she quickly shut me down with a stern: "No." Oh well I just chalked it up to her being from Brooklyn which made what I said to her the next time I saw her even more unexplainable. This time I saw her again walking down 6th Avenue, but accompanied by a young man.

I walked right up to her all confident like, nodded to the gentlemen, and went right into how I had read about her, and about her growing up in Jersey, and being childhood friends with Hope Davis. She looked at me, seemingly nodding in agreement, and said: "Right," and then they both walked off.

Something just didn't seem right afterwards, so the next day as soon as I got to a computer (I still had a "dumb" phone at this point) I IMDb'd her, and sure enough, I had cited Mira Sorvino's details to Marisa Tomei. She no doubt thought I was an idiot, and in that moment she probably was not too far off.

I have yet to have the opportunity to tell that story to Hope Davis, who also was a recipient of my album early on as well.

Talk about mistaken identities, I saw Elvis Costello out at the Blue Note one night with his wife. Now I had met Elvis early in my days of hustling. He rolled up eating an Italian icy so I gave him my record and asked him what he was working on. Real small talk kind of stuff, but it was cool. Since then I had seen him a few more times over the years so it became chill, meaning I had become somewhat accustomed to seeing him and so wasn't as star-stricken. I had never met his wife though. So I greeted him all nonchalantly, and waved him off, as if to say, I'm over you, and then proceeded to tell his Mrs. what a big fan of hers I was. Just as she thanked me I continued how I had really enjoyed that song of hers that was featured in that one movie, the title I couldn't recall at the moment, so I just said: "The one with Robert Duvall."

I immediately noticed a disconnection in her eyes, like I had brought the wrong plate of food to the table. She said, trying not to make me feel too awkward, that I had her mistaken.

I insisted that I wasn't mistaken; I mean who would know better about her identity, her or me?

She still said no, and she and Elvis just left the building, bidding me goodnight.

It kept eating at me, and then the name of the movie came to me, <u>Get Low</u> directed by Aaron Schneider, Sony Pictures Classic, 2009; and the singer was Allison Krause, not Diana Krall, who happens to also be a singer in her own right, and married to Elvis Costello. What do you know, who is back at the Blue Note, the very next night Elvis and his wife Diana Krall. So I was able to apologize for the mix up and explain myself.

She was gracious, and told me that it has happened to her often.

I appreciated her empathy, and did, shortly thereafter hear a couple of songs I like from Diana Krall, one even with Sir Paul McCartney,

I often times during this writing considered scrapping the whole idea. Especially in the early stages when I didn't have a clear direction of the narrative and or trajectory.

I simply didn't know where I was going with this. I figured nobody would be interested in reading about me meeting famous people, or worse that they would be overly harsh in their criticism.

This is due to the fact that even now in some of my everyday conversations with various people some or part of these accounts slip in to the conversation, I can't help it, you bring up a popular movie or T.V. show, and I'll probably have a story to tell you. Before long I could kind of sense some people's contempt, and it's not in my telling of the story I assure you.

Nobody likes a name-dropper, unless of course they're the name-dropper themselves. Oh they'll watch all the latest gossip, and numerous shows surrounding celebrities, but only as a guilty pleasure. You can't have celebrity without consensus, so if so many people don't really care about celebrities, then why are so many people famous?

Everybody wants to judge-nobody wants jury duty.

Sometimes I have just simply lost my nerve to approach a famous person for one reason or another.

Having something to offer somewhat quells the trepidation, but the fact remains, you know that people are watching, not so much you, but the person of interest.

Dave Chappelle literally turned his back on me in front of a long line of people who stood waiting outside the Blue Note one night.

I would see him up close and personal just moments later in the VIP room at the Blue Note. This was during the Rakim show and I simply nodded to him, with no hard feelings, because I learned that sometimes the contribution a person makes is greater than the moment in which you may meet them-Spike Lee taught me that at a screening for his movie <u>25th Hour</u> Buena Vista Pictures, 2002; and to top it off, that night, I even had on a Knicks hat.

I can only imagine though the difficulties and indifference he faces, trying to bring his visions to fruition, so it may be a little un-nerving to have so many people appear to care about your art so much now-so I forgive him.

One night as Salman Rushdie stood outside of the Blue Note awaiting entry. The line was somewhat long and I don't think the door guy recognized him. Naturally he was very conscious of his surroundings, and because I had on a long black leather coat I noticed him and his companion taking notice of me.

I was after all dressed like Shaft, and although I know Shaft went to Africa, I wasn't sure what his take on Islam was, so I just didn't approach Mr. Rushdie.

I was still in my teens when his book <u>The Satanic Verses</u>, Viking Press, 1988; came out, and never fully understood what the whole controversy was about, even up until recently.

I had watched him, not long before then, on NYC Media on television at the 92nd Street Y, talking about his books and some of his past experiences. And I didn't want to cause him anymore anxiety, due to the fact that I would have had to approach him from behind, without any discernible good opening line, or worse, call out his name. Although I disagree with his view on God's existence, he being such a staunch atheist, I did want to share with him how something that he said during the taping at the 92Y program helped me to appreciate the Bible even more. He said: "Books survive, because people love them." The Bible tells us that: "Love never fails" and that: "God is love," and that his word never fails. It is that same Spirit, and spirit of love that has preserved the Holy Scriptures down to this day.

One day while visiting with my son at his grandmother's house, who is affectionately known as "Mama;" my son's mother serves me with child support papers. She tells me that she was not supposed to be serving me directly, but that her sister, who was also there at the time, didn't want to get involved. Although we had not been a couple for some time we had a pretty good working relationship when it came to my son. My son had been with her, and her family since birth, and she bore the brunt of the responsibility of raising him, and taking care of his needs. The way she presented them to me though seemed like more a formality than anything. Once at the hearing though, everything changed. I don't even recall the initial date, but what I do recall is not feeling that denigrated since I sat before the parole board years back. The Magistrate, who was not surprisingly, a woman, read me the riot act. She gave me an ultimatum pay up, or go to jail. It was as if I hadn't done anything for my son, and was nowhere to be found since he was born. She judged me according to the papers that she had in front of her, and I didn't look good on paper (interestingly enough the term "on paper" is also a term offenders use to denote being on parole). The judge calculated my expenses based on my wages as a waiter, even though I explained to her that I was no longer able to wait tables because of a chronic skin condition. I guess they must hear it all because she wasn't trying to hear anymore, at least not from me. When I left the courthouse I was livid. I headed right for the train, and then thought it better to walk it off. So I walked up to Canal Street, then down to, and up Broadway. Once I got to 8th Street I hung a left heading west toward 6th Avenue. I figured since it was still early, I might as well get a good start on the day. The rest of the fellas would probably be showing up in the next hour or two. I was still trying to dismiss the dark cloud that lay over me from court, when right at 8th Street and 5th Avenue, I ran into Harvey Keitel. I immediately forgot all my troubles in that moment. I smiled at him as he walked in my direction, said hello and introduced myself. I mentioned to him that I was an artist as I handed him my music. I told him that I was a fan of his work, and I added: "Not just the stuff you did with Tarantino." I asked him what he was currently working on, and he said in an almost Deniro-esque fashion: "Some things." He had a dark Navy Pea Coat on, and I tell you, he was as cool as a fan. I didn't even ask him for a donation. It sometimes seems, even to me, disingenuous to ask someone for money, especially after complimenting them. Within a year though, this time on a Friday night, while a group of us stood in front of Fat Beats I saw Harvey Keitel walking down 6th Avenue this time with, I assume his wife. I had regretted not asking him for something for the album, not so much because of the money, but because from my experience, when someone gives you something, in the way of value for your music they're more likely to listen to it. That goes for millionaires as well. Before ever meeting Mr. Keitel me and my boy Rocco over the years would regularly recite the "Winston the Wolf" scene, and others scenes from <u>Pulp Fiction</u> written and directed by Quentin Tarantino, Miramax, 1994. I can't tell you how many times in an unrelated conversation, we'd just go right into it. To top it off, Harvey and his lady were even dressed in evening wear and it was her who grabbed my album from me and enthusiastically said that she wanted it. I looked at him, as if throwing the proverbial ball into his proverbial court. Not wanting to dampen his wife's enthusiasm, and just about two seconds before I was about to just give it to her for free, he reached into his pocket. I thanked them both, and then they were off.

I remembered thinking how unusual it was to see such a high profile actor walking down the street especially on a Friday night in NYC. More and more though I would see celebrities with varying degrees of fame, some super, others not as much, some eliciting stares and whispers, others going completely undisturbed, and unbothered, except of course by me. On my way to a following Child Support court date, I stuck my head into Hamish Linklater's movie-trailer which was parked a couple of blocks away from the court house, to say hello and to tell him what a big fan I was of his.

New York City: Daydreams & Pernoctations (Shouts to Ann Grifalconi-something a little bird told me)

Noted journalist and author Pete Hamill said in a discussion between himself and his esteemed colleague Tom Wolfe, something to the effect; that if you want to write about a city, any city, you must walk it.

Even before watching that discussion between writers on NYC Media, taped at the 92Y in NYC, I had gained an appreciation for walking the streets of New York. I've walked Manhattan's width, and almost its length, and if I knew the layout and contours of the other Boroughs I would walk them as well, and I suspect that I will. Let's face it though; you don't want to walk in the wrong neighborhood in any of the Boroughs, that aside I find myself walking the streets of NYC regularly.

Walking in Manhattan during the day can feel like you're surfing on waves of people, unless of course you find yourself in Time Square during peak hours, then it can feel more like quicksand. For the most part I try to avoid the tourist traps, because they're not only traps for tourist. Not that I've become a xenophobe or snob for that matter, seeing that I myself at one time was just an awestruck visitor here having only lived in New York City since around the turn of the Century.

I don't really care for some to the avenues, and streets, especially those with the same commercial paradigm of stores and franchises typical of any major metropolis, domestic, and even in some instances and distances- abroad. Union Square started to remind me of Amsterdam in spots.

Now even more especially with its drugstores, fast food- franchises, and shoe stores, eventually a neighborhood loses its individual charm. I feel frustrated at times amongst the throngs of folks trying to take it all in. I feel myself move with an arrogance found in the contempt of thinking you know a place. Taking for granted the same sights and sounds that I at one time was so taken in by.

Waves of people, almost as impersonal and driven as ocean waves themselves, pushed and pulled along by the lunacy of it all. The ebb and flow pulling you back and forth as you lay a washed in the tide. Both the waves and the current giving little or no thought to a part. When one droplet is displaced, another fills its place, one evaporates another precipitates. The cycle seems unchanging in this ever changing sea of humanity.

I recall the scene in the film <u>Closer</u>, directed by Mike Nichols, and written by Patrick Marber, Columbia Pictures 2004; where Natalie Portman's character finds herself walking up what appears to be the same bustling New York City street that she walked on in the film's outset, indiscriminately getting right back in where she fits in.

Movies play such a big role in NYC, and I find that so apropos because in no other place has my life felt so much like a movie, surreal like a dream, a hallucinatory haze- surreal as if walking through a maze replete with tastes, sights and sounds.

New York City provides a window through which one can shop for one's dreams. Though often only a one way mirror, where dreams can be seen, but the dreamer remains unnoticed by the dreams themselves. No vantage only a vista of being on the outside looking in or vice versa; and as with any window- even in the most illustrious of store-fronts, the light eventually dims, because there is no window as considerable, or as conservative as the window of time.

So you will yourself back to sleep, hoping to dream, yet again, yes, and maybe to even pick up where you left off dreaming. It's part exhilarating, part frustrating, like a film plot that doesn't quite go where you wanted, or expected it to go and so your attention diverts, but you're too time- invested to just cut your losses, so you continue to watch, and see it through.

New York has been the location of some of the world's most famous films, and filmmakers, and of those in the making. Its picturesque bridges, towering structures, and cavernous haunts where one can both lose and discover one's self and others, frequented by the many who dream about living here upon first sight, even if only in their dreams.

Some say New York City is the city that never sleeps, but that's not entirely true. There are times between the hours of 3:30 a.m., and 5:00 a.m., when, on a Sunday, Monday or Tuesday that the City does in fact power-nap;

And so the city starts to stir, as the stages of her awakenings occur.

First an arm, then a leg, and before you know it she's up in full stride with the smell of bagels and coffee in the air.

In many ways she's an unforgiving city, and like opportunity itself she favors the prepared while seeming to scorn the many who are living from hand to mouth, being only months, weeks, and sometimes, just days away from being homeless.

I've been there on at least four different occasions, now working on my fifth. It's comparable to juggling while walking a tightrope, and as I watch and listen to the neophytes documenting, venting and lamenting in unison, I smile to myself because I've begun to suspect this exercise to be a cry for kinship, for those of us who find safety in shared struggles.

I wonder if maybe this perpetual scavenger hunt is, in itself, a rite of passage- the cost, to hop aboard the big city, for some.

The juxtaposition of extreme wealth and poverty is more apparent at different times and places in NYC.

In some neighborhoods like the East Village, you have multi-millionaires living adjacent to the Projects; sharing the same parks and open spaces, so close and yet so far in the despairingly distant gamut between the haves and the more than half- that have not.

When I think of the song "New York, New York," written for and sung by Liza Minnelli, for the film directed by Martin Scorsese, United Artist, 1977; of the same name- which was later popularized by Frank Sinatra; in particular the famous lyric: "If I can make it there, I'll make it, anywhere" and how it became the mantra for so many aspiring people, I would dare to say that if moving to New York

to follow your dreams was a crime, some of those very artists in discussion (John Kander & Frank Ebb) could be considered accessories-after the fact.

The rising rents, and cost of transportation and food, the level of competition and difficulty of putting the ends together, the hustle and bustle, the saturation of aspiring people all vying, rolling and skating pass, and over the ones who falter and fall, and for what?

A troublesome journey for those who can't seem to fly or even get off the ground, due to whatever reason, lack of fuel or lift, brought on by the weight of the struggle...

Yet every so often one sails to a new height, soaring if only for a moment refueled by the vapors of past successes, yours and others.

Everybody knows somebody who has struggled, is struggling, or will struggle- I wrote this in part for those people- and the people they know.

You come to the appreciation that it's the collective caliber of the people you find in NYC, whether visiting or staying for a while.

Could this be part of the reason why we fight just to stay here and fight? Some of the sharpest people can be found here, and no wonder- probably due to all that friction they've experienced between those rocks and hard places.

Just when you think you got New York pegged, she has a way of bringing you back to the realization that there are some actions, and reactions that cause you to simply say: "Only in New York."

Like the inebriated man sleeping on a bench in the subway. Coming out of his stupor only long enough to release himself from his zipper, and urinate in plain sight, and in close proximity to the people who had the nerve to sit next to him in the first place. Not even opening his eyes, and failing to illicit even much of a stare or shrug or sound from anyone, except from me, you see I laughed so hard I almost went myself, but in that laugh somewhere was a cry, a cry at how hard this city can make you. How it is that whatever gland or organ that regulates shock in a person's mind must somehow get shut down or become visceral here. So that nothing ever really seems to surprise people in New York. Besides, sometimes a good seat in the NYC transit system is one of the few things a homeless person has going for them.

When people would suggest to me, while I was pushing my music on the street that I should: "Get on the internet." I'd respond: "If you mean that I should put myself out there, and reach people from all over the globe, I'm already on the internet;" I'm surfing and networking all within the circuitry of this grid-New York City.

One day as I'm talking to this woman Ann, who I had initially met a few years back, she goes on telling me how impressed she is by my memory. She tells me about her mother who she then tells me was a remarkable woman with an excellent memory herself. Ann asks me if I was familiar with memory palaces. I replied in the negative, and then I went on to tell her about my mother, and about her good cooking, and eye for photography. Ann apologizes for not being able to pick up my album and worries that by talking to me she may be causing me to lose potential customers.

I reassure her that I wasn't losing anything and that I was truly enjoying our conversation. In fact I was gaining I added, because if people see her, an older white woman, talking to me, they may conclude that I may not be that bad after all.

Not that I didn't want Ann to pick up my album, in fact she had already picked up one of my albums some years back, the very first time we met. She just doesn't remember, and that's fine by me. Not that I was even trying to dupe her into buying another record from me; what I really wanted from Ann is what she was already giving me, and I her- conversation.

You see what I remembered about Ann was that she is an illustrator, and author, in other words she's a storyteller. This was around the time when I would make the decision to finally stop pushing the music I had been pushing, and concentrate more on my writing. I realized during our conversation that I was not only delighted by her stories, but she was also-with mine.

Ann is in her eighties and she grew up in New York, which means that she was coming of age as an artist in the 50's, and probably moving and shaking from the 60s onward. Good ages to be, especially during such an epic age of Art, Music, and Culture in New York City.

After some time Ann bids me farewell only to return minutes later, this time with a book; The Memory Palace of Matteo Ricci by Johnathan D. Spence, New York Viking Penguin, 1984. The book she had referenced earlier in our conversation. She hands it to me, and says it's a gift. I thank her sincerely, and asked her if she had a card or contact info. She only had one card and it written on, so I took a picture of her business card with my phone and then she was off again this time more enduringly.

What I didn't tell Ann and what she couldn't have known is that I wasn't going to read that book anytime soon, if ever.

Oh I've read plenty of books, some, repeatedly. However some months prior to running into Ann again, I realized that although I had read many books and some more than once, I hadn't read the Bible from cover to cover.

So I had decided not to read another book in its entirety until I had read the Bible. However just minutes after she walked away I also concluded that it would be rude for me not to at least read some of the book considering it was a gift. So as I stood there in front of the movie theater on 13th Street & Broadway I opened the book, resigned to read whatever page I opened to, so as to at least justify her generosity.

The page number I opened to was 161 and the contents dealt with two of Jesus' disciples while "On the Road to Emmaus". I was blown away, not only because I had recently read that account in my daily Bible reading, but also because part of my nightly routine for months had been to go peer through the window of this one gallery in the West Village.

So most nights after hustling I would head over to Smalls, a jazz club off of 7th Avenue, and after having my fill of jazz, I would head further down West 4th Street to a place called Galleri Sand that would by that time of night be closed.

I was always captivated by the paintings, and from my vantage point outside, I could only get a good look at maybe 5 of the paintings. "Scenes from the Second World War" by Vebjørn Sand, was what the heading next to the closest painting read. However several paintings depicting scenes from war, or wartime were hung around the space. One of a group of soldiers bunkered down in what looks like a partially destroyed building, one of the injured soldiers being attended to by another, while another soldier who kind of resembles Christopher Walken stands by.

Another painting, and the only one that faced me directly hung from about 40ft away, and it depicted what looked like an outside ceremony, and a noticeably well- dressed woman seated at the end of an aisle in company with other well-dressed men and woman. The woman wore a long scarlet coat, and adjacent to her-outside the row of people seated, is a German Shepard. The scene is reminiscent of Yalta and the meeting between FDR, Churchill, and Stalin.

Still another picture depicts men in military uniform around a table on which a solitary glass of red wine was placed in the middle. Some of the men seem to be looking at a newspaper or map, and one of the painted men upon inspection elicits the effect of noticing my approaching presence, and this can be felt by me as I look at the painting.

The painting that most caught my eye though, and the only one of its kind that I could see, was a picture that seemed to me to be of a person, arms outstretched ascending into the clouds. I presumed it was the account of the ascension of Jesus Christ, and night after night I would visit it, and I even read the account from my Bible as I stood there late one night.

As I approached the paintings on another evening, a couple, a man and woman, were already themselves admiring them, and the man commented that the painting in question might be the account of Elijah in the windstorm, but I pointed out that there was no chariot visible.

The page that I had turned to in the book Ann gave me was entitled "The Road to Emmaus;" and the account in the Bible is one of the few accounts of the resurrected Jesus before his ascension into heaven. It was something that I had thought about almost every night over the past several months before receiving that book from Ann.

I contacted Ann to tell her of my plans to complete this manuscript, and of my page and mind opening experience with the book she had given me, and after correcting my pronunciation of "Emmaus" she had nothing but encouraging words for me. It was Ann who also introduced me to the word Pernoctation and fittingly so.

I happened by Galleri Sand again recently, this time during opening hours, and I asked about the painting: "The Ascension;" I queried to one of the two young men. There were mostly new paintings, most of which I had never seen before. One of the two young men who were present, neither being either of the artists (who from what I understand are twin brothers) themselves, but one of the young men, who was the son of one of the artists, was at a loss at which painting I was referring to.

He flipped through a catalogue of paintings, and came upon the one I had inquired about. It wasn't of the ascension he explained, but of a bull dozer, bull dozing human corpses. I realized that regardless of the artist's original intent that the piece itself, like the tendency of art, took on, not death, but a life of its own.

When I compare notes and observations with some of your more notable artists, creators, and contributors of today and yesterday; and especially when they expound on the insights that they gained in a particular field. I find that often times I have gained similar insights but out in the streets. Although I may have never been associated with some of your more prestigious institutions, like the proverb says, "As iron sharpens iron, So one man sharpens his friend." It is people after all that must first make the institution. The institution of Slavery in America, without the African becomes just a bunch of hard work that nobody wanted to do.

Ann by her own admission is not a religious person, but still she recognized the value in it when I told her of my desire to read the whole Bible.

Lucas Machowski, another one of the filmmakers I met on 6th Avenue, who happens to be from Poland, and who in exchange for me giving him my record, agreed that if he liked any of it, to do a music video. Days later when we met to shoot the video, during the course of our conversation, as he told me of his travels around the world, I asked him, what was his favorite place that he had visited; Expecting to give him pause, but without even a pause he said: "India," I challenged: "What about Brazil?" Nope he said that India had the best vibe of all the places he had ever visited.

Now never having traveled to India myself, and only having recently watched a documentary on PBS about India, I understood what he said next.

He said that people in India are very reverential towards strangers; in fact he said they worship them. I had learned that poverty was rampant in India, and he explained that although they didn't have much, they didn't feel that they needed much.

In Greek, one of the original languages of the Bible, the word hospitality literally means "Kindness to strangers." So short of worshipping your neighbor, to love them, is in line with loving God and yourself.

One beautiful sunny afternoon as I was walking down 6th Avenue, I noticed a young man that I knew from around the neighborhood who we call Bomb Jiggie. Bomb basically lives on 6th Avenue. He hocks his wares on a table that he shares with his father- of books and other miscellaneous items.

Bomb who is also an emcee was sitting on one of two plush leather-back swivel office chairs right there on the sidewalk. The kind of chairs you might expect to find in the corner office of a high rise building.

He looked so comfortable that I asked him if I could sit on the other unoccupied one. He, after quickly reprimanding me for even asking, directed me to sit down. We sat there on the sidewalk as people kept filing by, going and coming home from work, and to and from various destinations.

As we sat there basking in the sun, and enjoying the breeze, I remarked out loud:" Man I wish I was a millionaire." Bomb looked at me, scoffed, and said: "You already are one," and swiveled away in his chair. It took a second for what he meant to sink in, but looking at him I sensed that he wasn't worried about much, and probably because he didn't have that much to worry about.

My father once told me of an old African proverb that goes: "The poor cannot sleep because they are hungry, and the rich cannot sleep, because the poor people are awake." I found out recently that the quote was from the once foremost and now deceased Nigerian economist Sam Aluko.

**

Back in 2007 Creature and another fellow hustler Preachermann were invited to go to Hawaii and perform. Having wanting to go to Hawaii for some time I asked Creature to put me in contact with the girl who was organizing the show; who I then called and asked her if she could accommodate me as well, if I could make it out there on my own. She said that she could, and so I had just under a week to buy the ticket, and I had no cash only a bag full of music. So I worked overtime to get up the money for the ticket, and right on schedule I was able to book the flight. My son's mother was kind enough to book it for me being that I didn't have a credit card. However I wouldn't make the flight though, you see in a night of recklessness I had sat underneath a staircase with some random girl I met, who was panhandling on St. Marks St. during a rainstorm, and I had my passport in my back pocket, my only form of ID at the time, and it got soaked. I had thought nothing of it, because the security at bars were still accepting it, soggy and all.

Just days before my flight I had to make temporary moving arrangements because I was also being evicted from my space in Washington Heights- this wasn't my first time either, I had brought a crack-head in the house, one morning as the family I rented from ate breakfast. Subsequently they told me the next day that they were expecting an unexpected visit from family from the Dominican Republic, and they needed the room, and so I had to move my things to my sister's house.

On the morning of my flight, and in the dead of winter mind you, I got up put on my velour suit, not to be fly, but to be comfortable while flying; slid on my straw hat, anticipating lots of sun, and headed out to the train. I got to JFK with only minutes to spare. As I approached the counter and handed the lady my passport, I immediately noticed the disapproval in her face, as her nostrils shriveled up-sort of like my passport.

She asked if I had any other forms of ID, and signaled for her co-worker, presumably to consult with her. They notified me that my passport was what they call "mutilated," and that it was not valid for flying.

I checked franticly for any kind of ID, and found nothing, not surprising though, because my not having ID was the only reason I was carrying my passport in the first place. So it was a no go on the flight the woman informed me with almost a hint of sick satisfaction in her voice, or so it seemed.

I wasn't even dressed for New York weather, and to think all I had to do was what the lady on the phone had told me when I called to make the arrangements: "Go to Motor Vehicle or even to the Welfare office and get ID."

I cried, no I wept right there in the airport, and then I called Katie, the girl who had organized the show, and explained my situation, but there wasn't anything she could do.

The salvageable thing, unlike my passport was, my ticket was still good for one year, so the very next year I boarded a plane, (that I almost missed by being late-mind you), and flew to Hawaii.

It was the first time that I had worn shades since the MTV days. I even hustled out in Waikiki, and sold out of music in just a matter days. I got to meet some of the island's musicians as well, and almost fell in love with a cellist from afar. I ate pancakes with boysenberry and coconut syrup for breakfast. I didn't see any whales though, which was one of my main reasons for ever wanting to go to Hawaii.

The musicians in Hawaii were so laid back in contrast to the ones back in New York. It irked me a little at first and then I figured out the reason why the musicians in Hawaii were so laid back, it's because they're already in Hawaii. Hawaii is the place where ambition goes to lose itself.

If ever you anticipate going to Hawaii, don't watch a whole week of Shark Week on the Discovery Channel, before you go out there, and then wear a big "Jaws" t-shirt on the beach- it probably won't go over well.

During the time I was out in Hawaii, Questlove also had a show advertised out there, but I didn't see him while in Oahu.

I had seen him on 6th Ave from time to time, at the health food store, and he would just nod, and keep it moving. He was on the do-not-call-out-to list as well, but mainly because of him being a DJ, drummer for The Roots, and a label owner, and besides, he would just give us a look like, please, and not the polite way either. I'm thinking maybe I should have made more of an effort to schmooze him although he didn't seem like he even wanted to be schmoozed.

Some years later I would go down to the Kidrobot store in SoHo, for an event in which Questlove was the DJ. An emcee called Deca, along with his girl Darah, and I had met up with Deca's boy DJ, Stan, and his lady.

Deca and I, along with some others, ended up performing that night backed by Questlove on the turntables, it was a good night, and

I still had my own show to attend later that evening at the Bowery Poetry Club.

Questlove is also a big inspiration for this writing. Some years back I had seen online where he had a bunch of blocks with individual celebrity names on them; when you'd clicked on the block, up popped an amusing anecdote about Quest and the person on whom you clicked.

Questlove I've heard has since written a couple of books which I have not yet read, but maybe I'll take a gander at them one day. I would expect him to meet a lot of people, and have many interesting stories to tell, because of his high profile; nonetheless I think I read each one of those blocks in one sitting.

Creature himself wrote a book, The Underdog's Manifesto: A Guerilla Artist's Path to Independence, Outskirts Press 2007, along with writer Dax Devlon Ross, which also started my literary juices to flowing. It's good to be around people who are doing things they're passionate about, it can empower and encourage you, and it should.

In the streets of New York acknowledging an actor and a role they have played, at times was almost the equivalent of acknowledging the city of an individual who you have met. Knowing the least little bit about where someone is from is tantamount to knowing part of their identity, even if it's only the name of the city or town. People who said they were from Norway were impressed when I asked: "Oslo?" Just like a Portuguese person when I queried: "Lisbon?" The more obscure their city may have seemed to them, in comparison to New York, the more impressive my responses were, even when I was off, it usually was not by far, and even if it's by hundreds of miles, it was still closer than not knowing that a place even exists, which is a perception many foreigners have about Americans, and more specifically New Yorkers- that we are near-sighted when it comes to the outside world.

As a waiter you learn to embellish dishes, especially the specials. Now although that might sound redundant, it is often the specials that the chef/cook wants to see go first. As the chef of my own music, I also learned to use terms that enhance. So like when butter becomes "shaved butter," my songs became "crafted compositions." After all, like any chef, I want all my dishes (discs) eighty-sixed. I used words like "infused" and "sprinkled" (thanks Scram), which speaks to the relationship between music and food. I often tell folks: "I look at music like food; I don't care where it comes from, as long as it's good."

I met Chef Thomas Keller as he strolled passed me on West 3rd Street one evening. Unlike Mario Batali, I at first had no idea who he was, that is, in the culinary scheme of things. Of course Mario Batali is on television regularly and so more recognizable.

When I first met Mr. Batali it was on 14th Street, and as he was about to leave on his scooter I approached him and told him that my music was like "gnocchi with truffle sauce" He replied as he took my album: "It's sexy, and delicious, and I love it," and then he rode off. What struck me about Chef Keller though, when I met him was how he handed me his business card like it was money. Each time after when I would periodically organize the business cards I had accumulated, I'd always ponder over his. I've seen some pretty fancy business cards; but was intrigued by how such a simple business card had been handed to me like currency. Still unaware of his renown, a year or two later, I heard someone allude to him while watching Charlie Rose on PBS. Shortly thereafter Chef Keller himself, along with one of his protégés, was a guest on Charlie Rose, and it struck me how a man, who was that accomplished, still walked around handing out business cards.

One day as I stood on 6th Avenue, and I must tell you, it was one of those days. Two women walked by me, and as I offered my CD to the one, she accepted it, but upon my mentioning of money, she hands it back to me saying: "Oh no, I don't want to pay for that." The other woman however looked at me, and said benevolently: "I'll take it." After she paid me, and took the record, I asked her for her name, and she replied: "Dana" and I quickly returned: "You're Dana Delany- I loved you on China Beach;" the television drama that aired on ABC; One instance of recognition begat another.

A Writer in My Own Right- Right?

Years ago a writer wanted to do a piece on us for <u>The New York Times</u>, but after asking him a few pointed questions, I declined. Not that I don't respect the paper or its readers and subscribers, I just didn't want to pull back the curtain on my fellow artists who were still out there hustling.

Whereas some of the other guys may have seen it as a good opportunity, being in the "NY Times" in all, I felt it could do more harm than good. Especially from some of my experiences while dealing with the sort of people who considered themselves "informed;" I definitely didn't want to be marginalized.

I could already imagine hearing people tell me: "Oh yeah I read about you guys in <u>The Times</u> I know what you're all about." In fact I didn't even have to imagine it, we had all heard similar expressions before from people who may have had a bad experience with another person on the street, or read somebody's blog.

Even as people would approach sometimes I could see the supposedly, more savvy of the bunch schooling the other(s) as to what to expect from us as they walked in our direction. Even at times physically blocking or pulling the curious person away from us, as if they were rescuing them from certain death, which always irked me.

Not only for the obvious reasons, but also because some of those people were depriving their friends, and relatives of a pretty unique experience. I've received messages from all over the planet from people who've either picked up my record, or were somehow connected to someone who picked it up while in New York or wherever.

I had become part of their NYC memorabilia-a link to a place that people visit, for among other reasons, for the memory, and now to have a story to tell their friends, and a soundtrack; there are few interactive artistic experiences that cost so little.

Just the thought of being in on the ground floor of an artist seeking to establish themselves, I must tell you people spend more money on lottery tickets, despite astronomical odds, just to be able to imagine, if only for a little while, "what if;" The probability never being a factor. To some to live vicariously, is still to be living.

So in part I'm writing this for those that supported me; to justify their purchases, and whatever boasts they may have made in my behalf. Even when growing up in Utica to have friends and family who lived in New York City was viewed as a privilege, something to be said with pride.

New York is celebrated in part because of its past, its present, and it-that is, the future is here. New York City is the kind of place where you can experience time travel without breaking the space-time continuum. That might be a bit much, but that's New York isn't it?

It's easier to put people in a nice neat little box, even if that box is a movie, television screen, magazine, and yes even a book, only to be circular filed later, when people tire of their stuff; Rather than to explore and discover something or someone that may inspire or challenge you.

A pleasurable paradox for me was when someone was actually surprised that they liked my music. Like my son in the theater that day, sometimes if people don't associate you with the big time, well then, you just ain't what's popping.

When some presumptuous type would say to me: "Oh you want five dollars for your CD right?" I would sometimes be inclined to respond: "It's more than just a CD, it's my music, my art, and I just wanted to share it with you for a price that we can both live with;" live being the operative word; it's really not all about dollars and cents.

I turned down what was touted to be a lucrative opportunity just to perform, along with my sister, Ms. Jerri Lorell, for a quarter of what I was projected to make out of town.

It was to perform at a conference held On August 9 and 10th, in 2007 at CUNY's John Jay College of Criminal Justice in New York, N.Y. entitled; "On the Edge: Transgression and the Dangerous Other." The keynote speaker was Amiri Baraka, and the opportunity of being on the same bill as Mr. Baraka, even if it wasn't a bill, was one I just couldn't pass up. It was worth more than even what they paid me, or what I could have made if I had gone to Cincinnati. It was the privilege to stand alongside history, but in the present tense. Besides, what can five dollars buy you today anyways? I have to be consistent with the market.

Industry people, as we call them, sometimes like to give the impression to the impressionable that in order for it to be considered "real" work or art of any value it must be quantifiable. The reality is that often an aspiring artist of any age is, by virtue of aspiration, more inclined to be impressionable.

So that being the case, often opportunities for collaboration with some of these want-to-be artists who've adopted this false point a view is stagnated, because of their perception of what constitutes a respectable profitable project.

HELLO- most of us have done, what we do for free up until this point, and even beyond and will continue to do so.

A guy named Moe once told me: "Most business deals are done at night, in bars and restaurants-the paperwork just gets done during the day." So a guy like me, with no big company behind me was relegated often times to having meetings with people, about having meetings, which at that rate left me two steps behind in the process of getting things done, but I soldiered on.

People don't want to pay you what you're worth anyway so I worked not just to get paid, but so that even after I got paid, I could continue to work. I never felt like I was working while promoting on the streets. That's not to say it was easy by any stretch of the imagination. We made it look easy, because it was what we were passionate about. What artist doesn't want to live off their art? It was my belief at one point that either you made it "big" or you were nothing. I know now that there is so much space, in between the dials of superstardom, and being a working musician, and many of the working musicians that I know are more than happy to just be working, even if not being as recognizable as some of the stars with whom they often work with.

I met Kristen Schaal of HBO's *Flight of the Conchords* fame, and various other projects that I'm sure she might just as well like to be defined by. She walked passed me on West 3rd Street, and as I offered her my album, she tried to be all cutesy about telling me no. So I had to dig into my sales bag, and change the subject to what and who she likes to listen to.

In sales we were encouraged to ask people non-sales related questions, like about the weather and such. Now some people will tell you that they hate the question: "Who is your favorite;" in regards to this or that? I think, however that often people love those kinds of questions, but hate not to seem like the answer is a simple one, so as to maintain their air of dimensionless, and appear to be the wide-ranged individuals that they envision they are. So when someone gives me a hard time about answering those kinds of questions, I whittle them down to that particular day or week or who it was that they last listened to.

Kristen Schaal's answer was Tori Amos, and without missing a beat, I went into my, something-left-to-be-desired, rendition of, "Butterfly," a song by Tori Amos that I once listened to a lot, from the soundtrack of the movie <u>Higher Learning</u>, directed by John Singleton, soundtrack by Epic Records, 1995, when I had a little time on my hands.

Now I was a little iffy on the lyrics, but she seemed impressed enough so then I asked her if she knew that Tori Amos was a fan of Eminem's music. Then I went back to humming the song, missing lyrics and all-garbling crescendos at each last lyric of each verse, and when she laughed, so did I, because it was funny, and when you can make a comedian laugh, you're as we say, in there.

After that she asked me, somewhat cautiously: "How much for the CD?" Now from my experience, and by the tone of her voice, and phrasing of the question I assumed that the issue I was dealing with could very well be her not having much cash on hand.

So I told her that Mary Louise Parker had bought my record earlier that day, for a fair price that she and I both agreed on; Because unless you advertise price most people have no idea what you, as the artist, are expecting as far as compensation for your work goes.

Plus because it's your work and you'll more likely than not, place a higher value on it, they don't want to offend you either. So I stress to people that it's more about the support and the gesture than necessarily what they can give me at that time. Plus I invite them, if they feel so inclined, to come back and throw a couple of more bucks my way. People tend to carry less cash nowadays anyways.

Kristen Schaal picked up the record and then I asked her if she had ever met Tori Amos. She said no, and I encouraged her to use some of her rising star power to pull some strings to meet Tori Amos, and I smiled at the thought of Kristen telling Tori Amos what had transpired between her and I.

The whole bit about Mary Louise Parker was true; she had picked up my record within a few hours of Kristen. The first time I ever spoke to MLP though was in front of Fat Beats a few years prior, and in hushed tones. She was pushing a stroller with, I assume her sleeping child inside, with her nanny or assistant in tow, but it was not to be that day or for many days after, because every time I would see Mary she'd be in a rush, whether coming or going, and never really at an opportune time.

However me being the shooter, and the shooter always having a shot, I figured I'd just have to wait for mine; and it came when earlier that night, before I met Kristen, I was posted up outside of that same Barnes & Noble that used to be on the corner of 6th Avenue and 8th Street.

I saw Ms. Parker exit out of the book store, and after a short while, she kept peering in through the store window, as if she was waiting for someone. She was within earshot of me so I said hello, and then added: "You know you and I have a mutual friend?" Before she could ask who, I continued: "Adam Duritz." I had read that they were friends, and I was, you could actually say, friendly with Adam.

Her face and tone quickly warmed up, and so I showed her my album, and gave her a quick synopsis, and then I asked for the sale. She perused through her purse, gave me some money, and excused herself saying that she had to look for her boyfriend. I mentioned in the most matter-of fact-dead-pan-tone I could muster, that I was single. She laughed, but in an appreciative way, I hope. I thanked her for her support, and as she walked away I yelled out to her that I had really appreciated her recent contributions to Esquire magazine, and I had.

At the now defunct car company Saturn we were taught to describe the features, overview, and benefits, of the vehicle before asking for the sale. The idea is that you have to earn the right to ask for the business. Conversely, if as a waiter, you perform all 12 points of service before dropping the check, the whole process goes smoothly, and plus now you free up the table for more guests and more often than not yield good tips and repeat business. Saturn was all about repeat business, and recommendations, because they understood the value of the customer (guest) extended far beyond just the one transaction, just as buying a car is more than writing a check. Word of mouth is an important aspect of any business. People have developed businesses solely based on the accumulative word of mouth.

I first met Adam Duritz kind of, as I was coming out of the Dallas BBQs restaurant that at one time was located at University Place & 8th Street. There was a small group of us and we were being somewhat rambunctious probably due in part to partaking of the Texas size drink specials for lunch.

I called out his name as he passed, but he just kept it moving saying something about being on the phone which he was, but what I wanted to tell him was: "I want to talk to you too Adam." I understood though, even when we ran into Bookeem Woodbine just moments later, he wanted nothing to do with us either.

A couple of weeks later, I saw Adam again, this time on 6th Ave, and he was carrying a brand new umbrella, I started to speak to him, and he nodded me off, like a pitcher on the mound, with a full count. As he passed me though I just started belting out: "It seems like I should say, as long as this is love, and it's not always easy so maybe I should…" which are lyrics to one of my favorite songs from him, entitled "Anna Begins." As he continued to walk and just when I started to think he wasn't going to stop he did. He made an about face, and walked right back up to me, and said the two words I like to hear: "How much?" He posed it, not like a question though more like an ultimatum.

He picked up my record and even had me as his guest at some of his shows which were always entertaining and fun. I even got to see him at the Borgata in Atlantic City.

Adam is a good guy and not your average rock star type. In fact I may have offended him when I suggested that he invoke more of his rock-star power, while we were entering the after party inside the casino.

Once again, it was people, in this case me, pretending to be people, who they are not. Adam said later in an interview I watched, that: "Fame is not something that you do; it's what people do to you." I had recalled listening to "August and Everything After" by the Counting Crows when it was first released years ago. I wanted to be him in the way I thought that he, as he sings in one of his songs: Wanted to: "Be Bob Dylan." The little I got to know him I can tell you that he just really wants to be himself.

Adam's song "Anna Begins," from the album, *August and Everything After*, Geffen, 1993; would also be the tie that bound me with Anna Paquin; in a conversation that is. I literally almost ran into her, in the produce aisle at Life Thyme. She was lovely right from the start. I told her that I had enjoyed her performance in <u>The Squid and the Whale</u> directed by Noah Baumbach, Samuel Goldwyn Films, 2005. I asked her if she had ever got a chance to meet Laura Linney.

I told her I had seen Laura in passing but didn't talk to her much. Then almost forgetting my manner of making a living, I showed her my album and gave her a quick description and she readily agreed to pick one up.

I sung a little of "Anna Begins," before asking her if she knew it, and her smile let me know that she did even before the word yes came out of her mouth. This was before she was married and even before her series on HBO, became a big hit. She was one of the sweetest-most genuine people, famous or not, that I have met- her and Joss Stone.

Like I express to people some of the time, even if one of my inspirations, picks up my record, and just has it lying around in his or her house I'm happy. The guy named Beef who sort of mentored, and managed me early on, told me one day after having not seen him for years, that he saw my album inside Russell Simmons' Maybach.

Beef used to work with Russell, and Russell had picked up my album some years before. So when some hot shot rapper or rocker like the drunken drummer from a fairly new band wants to try and pull rank, I tell them: "If Russell Simmons could buy my album you can too." Because if there is anybody that could legitimately guilt or should I say impose upon me to give them my music for free, it would be Russell Simmons. He not only is a pioneer in Hip Hop, but he pioneered a whole movement, and is responsible directly or indirectly for many of the heavy weights in Hip Hop and by extension other genres today.

Now mind you, I'm not a singer per se, but as far as being able to hold a note goes some days are better than others. As a songwriter and I think most songwriters will agree, the thought of people singing your songs is an inspiration in itself. When you sing an artists' song back to them, be it at a show, on the street, or in a grocery store, it lets the artist know that the song made a connection. Maybe that's where in part the term "hit" came from in the music biz, before a song hits the charts it has to hit the hearts, or minds of the masses, just like a "hook" is supposed to grab you and then idealistically manifest monetarily. When an artist takes time to craft a song, weaving its fabric and smoothing its texture, his or her hope is that someone will at least put it on.

One thing I learned in the car business which was contrary to what I had thought was conventional wisdom, was that although the man does, more often than not, wear pants; In matters of business, especially within a marriage setting, it is often the woman who wears "the pants." So in order to get a leg up, so to speak, you need the wife's consent. Naturally, because buying a car is usually the second most expensive purchase a couple will make after buying a home. In the process of selling a car, if a man says he needs to consult with his wife, you best believe, that is what he needs to do. Now of course there are exceptions, but as a rule, you put a halt to all paperwork until the wife has been consulted, and confirms the purchase of the vehicle. Or you risk an angry wife followed by a defeated looking husband bringing you the keys to the car back to the dealership and slamming them on the desk.

All my job training and especially much of the training I received at home has benefited me. One case in point happened on a Sunday afternoon in front of Fat Beats. Being that the record store was only open for a few hours on Sunday, and Sundays in general were often slower, due probably to people trying to fully depressurize before the pressure of the next day. I tried to make every effort count- especially on Sundays.

As I'm standing in front of the record store a group of kids roll up with a woman, and as the first kid, a young man heads upstairs, I offer him my album, giving him a brief overview of the music and production. After which I asked him if he'd like to pick up a record. Just then, the woman, who I assume is the mother of one, if not all of the teenagers, chimes in and says: "Don't you think you should wait and see what you can get upstairs?" Now if I'm talking to an adult, and another adults starts running interference, I immediately isolate that one adult, sometimes even with, say a line from a movie, for example Joe Pesci's character's line in Martin Scorsese's <u>Goodfellas</u>: "Whoa Anthony he's a big boy;" screenplay by Nicholas Pileggi, Warner Bros, 1990. Whether it's a man or woman who was being intrusive, they usually got the point.

However much I needed to make a sale that Sunday afternoon, I restrained myself from so much as even shooting the woman a dirty look. Despite her reasonable suggestion to wait, the young man agreed to pick up my record right then and there, and I thanked them all as they went up into the record store, and when they came back out just minutes later, I bid them farewell as they walked away.

Just then, this kid Jose who worked at Fat Beats walks up, and says to me: "You see who that is over there, over there, by Grays Papaya, it's Paul Simon." I quickly collect my bag, and myself and head towards the corner which was only yards away.

As I approached Mr. Simon I smiled, and without even saying hello I started singing some of the lyrics to one of his songs, "The Vampires." From his album <u>Songs from The Capeman</u>, Warner Bros. 1997, taken from the Broadway musical he produced called, *The Capeman*. As I'm doing this, the kid who had just bought my album just minutes before, along with the other kids, and the woman all converge around him, and I realize that they're his family. The mother is, I assume, Edie Brickell, a singer in her own right; both singers whose songs, I have actually referenced in my very own songs.

The boy who had patronized me then compliments me on even knowing the song I sung in part to Mr. Simon, because as he said most people only know the more popular songs. I go on to tell Mr. Simon about how my boy Richie and I would sit in his apartment listening to all kinds of music including his, and so I asked Mr. Simon if he'd say hello to Richie on the phone. He agreed and I made the call, but Richie didn't pick up so Mr. Simon was kind enough to leave him a message.

I don't even like to think how different things may have gone if I was rude at the outset. When I approached Mr. Simon he was actually talking to a man who, I kid you not, could've been Julio from down by the school yard. Then I went back to my perch, and watched as they all stood around for a bit, and curiously enough the only other person that came up and said hello to Paul Simon, while I looked on, was an older black woman.

Sometimes it's the people that you almost, but don't quite meet, that stick with you. I completely lost my cool when Tracee Ellis Ross walked passed me up 6th Avenue. I basically became a bumbling idiot-mumbling gibberish. I tried desperately to use my words but in doing so I alarmed her even further. I was like a choking victim, and she, somebody who didn't know how to perform the Heimlich or CPR. She walked away hurriedly, saying apologetically: "Sorry sir;" yeah, Ms. Ross, you know what you did.

Over the years I've pushed my body to the limit as far as the elements go; I stood out in the hottest heat for as long as I could take it, and then some, and then, with the same determination, in the coldest cold. Sometimes hung over, hungry, and itching with bouts of being weak in the bladder. Often people supported me just because I was out there. People were more likely to buy an album when it was very cold, as opposed to it being very hot. New Yorkers and this may hold true for people in other cities as well, take a day or two to adjust to any weather condition. They experience what I like to call weather-shock. Once they get acclimated though they're back to their ole charming selves. Besides you can do more about the cold than you can about the heat as far as clothing goes. When it's frigid you can easily and more appropriately make adjustments in just how much clothing to wear. People get hot and bothered easily in the summer and don't even want to talk, and if it rains all week after just a day or two people are usually unfazed by the rain.

On cold days in New York people sometimes act like they never expected this kind of weather in the Northeast.

On one such cold day, and I mean it was cold, the kind of cold that could provoke one to cursing. I happened to be standing; you guessed it, in front of the Blue Note. That night I had moved closer to the door than usual to shorten the distance between me and the patrons so as to be quicker on the draw. The door guy was not standing outside as usual because of the cold and another guy who I had never seen at the door before, kept going in and out in intervals, and at times looking at me, only to go back inside.

This went on a few times, and I began to think that maybe he was a cop, but he wasn't dressed like a cop. He had a cashmere coat on, no hat and suede shoes, and if memory serves I believe they were blue. Amel Larrieux was playing that night and I had on a snorkel, long johns, and thermal socks, and I was still freezing. So I knew that this dapper gentleman had to be cold. When he wasn't outside he was at the plate glass window looking out toward the street. I figured he was waiting for somebody of importance, and the next time he came out, this time with the door guy, I overheard him say that his "subject" would arrive in 15 minutes.

About 30 minutes later a limousine pulls up right in front, and out hops Prince. As he moved quickly toward the door and in my direction all I could think to say was: "Oh snap, Prince;" he froze in mid stride, one knee up with one knifed hand pointed north and the other south; he reminding me of the Heisman Trophy, sort of as he looked me directly in the face, unfroze and then walked inside the club never saying a word, and yet I can't think of a better way to kind of meet Prince-sort of.

He was joined shortly thereafter by Hype Williams, who I gave my record to. Hype help revolutionize music videos and made them into mini- motion pictures, and then went on to direct a major entitled, Belly, Big Dog Films, 1998 starring, among others Nas, who picked up my record outside the Virgin Mega-store. Also Nas' father Olu Dara, a music legend himself, picked up my record on 6th Ave and even called to congratulate me on one of my shows, and to tell me that he and his horn couldn't make it to play with me that night.

Sometimes I tell people after talking for some time, that my CD makes a great conversation piece, and then I add: "You see what it's done for you and I already." I also like to use words like credenza which I picked up from my old new car manager Carlo, and if someone rejects my music with any degree of pomposity, I tell them: "Michel Legrand picked one up, and he's a maestro." Hey as they say: "A closed mouth doesn't get fed."

"Those who were there will remember."

When I would offer my music to people, and at times they'd say: "I'm not interested"; I'd sometimes reply in a semi-sarcastic, yet consoling tone: "I think you're very interesting;" as if I had misheard them. Then I might even go as far as saying how they shouldn't be so hard on themselves; that everyone is interesting in their own way, and I'd even start to point out some of the positive points I could obviously see about them.

It would be hilarious to me, to hear them trying to interject in between my rapid-fire rattling off of compliments, until they either conceded, or just walked away frustrated, especially if they fancied themselves trying to kill me with kindness. More often than not, it would be the other way around. Every so often though, I'd get the mind-your-own-business end of a verbal sparring match, but even then, it was entertaining to see, and usually made for a good laugh.

No city offers the various forms of verbal sparring like New York City, and so if I can keep a person talking, even if in an argument or a debate, I still have a shot and like I was once told: "A shooter always has a shot." That reminds me, I'll have to make a note to tell you about the time I literally lost my "hat" in a pool game.

During many of these instances with well-known people there were moments that I just couldn't help but recognize the simple humanity in people.

Chris Noth was at the Whole Foods in Union Square with his lady, and I didn't even think about approaching him, neither did anyone else from what I observed. You could tell that all he wanted to be was just a guy shopping for groceries with his woman, not Mr. Big, plus he had already picked up my record a year or so prior.

Sam Rockwell walked down 6th Avenue one misty afternoon with a broken umbrella, the kind of broken umbrella that even I would have probably second guessed going outside with, even in the rain.

The kind of umbrella that the street peddlers have on hand just for rainy days; you know the ones that the unprepared pedestrian must then buy although knowing the umbrella won't be good for many uses, and after trying to haggle, sometimes even in the midst of the downpour, end up buying anyways, because after all when the demand is great-the price is at the discretion of the supplier.

Although I've seen some defiantly refuse to buy them, either out of contempt, or principle. Throwing caution to the rain; and to me though the whole scenario had the makings of a Chinese proverb or an adage that could very well go: "Never try to negotiate for an umbrella in a downpour." I remember during the great Blackout of 2003 the price of a slice of pizza, at this one particular pizzeria on Avenue C, even selling for double.

The funny thing was- it didn't seem like the umbrella Sam Rockwell held had been recently broken either. It seemed like he actually left home with it in that condition, intent on getting his $5 dollars' worth. I got a good laugh though, and he picked up a record even after I mistook him for being in the <u>Singing Detective</u> (dir. Keith Gordon, Paramount Classics, 2003) when I actually meant <u>Confessions of a Dangerous Mind</u> directed by George Clooney, Section Eight Productions, 2002, based on <u>Confessions of a Dangerous Mind: An Unauthorized Autobiography</u>, originally published in 1982.

In any business where negotiations are involved it is not wise to negotiate from a position of weakness. To illustrate: One day while working as a sales consultant for the Saturn dealership in Poughkeepsie, this man walks into the dealership and after a brief introduction we then go and sit down at the table to discuss his automobile needs. Shortly thereafter he leans over and places a brick of cash on the table in the space that lay between him and me, and said simply: "This is all I'm willing to pay!" I could tell by his body language and grimace that he wasn't trying to hear the whole bit about how this was Saturn, and we don't haggle, in fact he wasn't interested in a Saturn at all. He owned a landscaping business, and so needed a van and it just so happened we had a used van that suited his needs almost perfectly.

I could tell you that the man was a redneck, but that could've been just because he spent so much time in the sun. He told me that among his many clients was James Earl Jones, and so I asked him how meeting Mr. Jones in person was. He replied that he dealt more with Mrs. Jones, and that she pulled no punches. I studied him as he sat there in jeans and a t-shirt and it became more apparent that he could care less about the "No haggle-no hassle" buying experience. He wanted what he wanted, and for how much he wanted it for, and so he decided to make a show of force.

I must say I was impressed by his brazenness, but when one works according to a process and steps are involved, one must decide even in the forgoing or side-stepping of the previous step, what the next step in the sequence is. Regardless of the step, the aim is always the same-control; whether you're dropping a check at a table, or the price on a used Dodge, you want to remain in control.

Right about then the used car manager Mike V walks by, and does a double take at me, the guy, and the stack of money on the table. I looked at Mike who was now halfway across the showroom, pointed my finger at the gentlemen across from me, and said loudly, and simply: "This man just used the N-Word."

Just as the air was being sucked out of the room, most of it into the lungs of all who gasped, I elaborated: "Negotiate." It was just enough to break the ice, and to take the fight out of the man, because any boxer or runner will tell you, no wind-no wins, now about that hat.

One night while I was at the Cherry Tavern over there near Avenue A, and 6th Street I started playing this guy, let's call him "Chad" in a game of pool. I had played Chad many times before over the years, and we all know Chad; even if you don't know this particular Chad, you know the type maybe- the camp counselor with the summer-camp-team-leader personality. The kind of guy who has been to one too many "principles of management" seminars, and the kind of guy that asks, even in ordinary dive bar conversation, questions like: "Is that okay?" Or: "Does that make sense?" After making any ole suggestion; in other words the kind of guy you don't want to lose to in a pool game.

Well I ended up losing 3, that's 3 games in a row, and we were playing for 10 dollars a pop. After the third game he didn't want to play anymore and neither did I, and it was pay up time. So I had to come clean about not having the money, and after giving me the camp counselor reprimand he suggested that I give him my hat as collateral until I had the cash. The hat was one of those authentic Crocodile Dundee styled hats that I had developed an affinity for. It fit me well, especially when traversing the concrete jungle of NYC. The fact that I didn't even have the $30 bucks to pay Chad meant that either; (1) I didn't work that day, (2) I worked but didn't make that much cash, or (3) and the more likely of the scenarios; I had wasted money on foolishness the night before and had slept in all day; The kind of foolishness that leads to losing your hat in a pool game. To make matters worse, I was sort of homeless at the time. I had been staying in a hostel in Brooklyn, and I didn't even have the 30 bucks to pay the nightly fee, and although I was broke I still found a way to get myself inebriated, and in no condition to take the train way out to Sheepshead Bay to crash at my boy Rocco's, like I had done on more than one occasion.

So what did I do? I went to Ray's Pizzeria on St. Marks, and as I'm sitting down at one of the outside picnic tables wishing I was in bed, any bed, even the bed bug infested cot at the hostel would've been welcomed at that point. Just then a yellow cab pulls up, and the driver, an African guy, hops out and walks quickly into the store on the corner. I mean he left the cab running right there in front of me. Without a moment to waste I got up, and as I approached the cab I felt a feeling of exhilaration start to build inside my chest. As I opened the door and slid behind the steering, wheel my excitement heightened, enough even to seemingly sober me up, if only for a moment. As I put the car in gear, my exhilaration dissolved into euphoria, which is the only way I can describe what I felt. I realized in that moment as I was pulling off, that barring me getting into an accident or something worse, it would be very unlikely that the police would be inclined to screen every cab that rode passed them, checking each license plate, and numbers. So I took my pre-paid phone out of my pocket and dialed Rocco's number, and when he picked up, barely awake, I asked him how to get to his house, "driving?" He asked, still half asleep: "Where are you?" I answered, trying to choke back a laugh: "In a cab;" as I sucked the snot back into my nose and back into my mucous membrane.

When I arrived at the apartment I told my boy Wicz, who roomed with Rocco at the time, that: "I just literally took a cab." He didn't believe me at first but later that day as we left to go to the deli I showed him the cab parked right in front of the apartment building and although he was still skeptical, as the next day, and then as the next couple of days passed, and as the cab accumulated parking tickets, he finally started to believe me. I had parked the cab purposely near a fire hydrant, reasoning that it would be quickly discovered and returned to its owner. I even called a random cab company and asked the dispatcher hypothetically what punishment, if any, a driver would receive for his car getting taken for a joyride? The guy told me that the driver would more than likely just be given another car, and would have to wait for the missing car to resurface. Re-surface, huh, I thought, how fitting, especially considering that at that moment I had once again hit rock bottom.

I'm Not Supposed to be here.

Like somebody once told me: "There are two sides to every story, and then there's the truth." Here's my side of the story- I had been hanging out in Williamsburg, which we sometimes affectionately and contemptuously referred to as, Billyburg. My boy Wicz, had ended up meeting this guy named Conrad when they both were working at a music shop near Time Square. Wicz and I had roomed together in the Bronx after I first arrived in New York. So I would spend a lot of time at Con's studio on Hope Street in the Williamsburg section of Brooklyn. Sometimes I spent days there, and because the studio was in a warehouse styled building and had no windows, sometimes it was hard for me to decipher when I finally emerged, if it was indeed 6am or 6pm. I used to party pretty hard I must tell you.

One night Con played me this song called "Chemo Limo" by an artist named Regina Spektor, and I fell in love with the music and the song. I listened to it numerous times while in the studio, and played it for as many people as would listen.

I had read somewhere that she was from Russia, but had moved to the Bronx at an early age. What made me even more enamored with her was that she had also frequented The Sidewalk Café, which is right across the street from the Pyramid Club, on Avenue A, which as you may remember, happens to be the venue, and main scene I had come up in. We would often go and shoot pool at the "Sidewalk" after the open mic. I had saw Kaki King and a lot of talented though lesser known artists play at the Sidewalk Café over the years, and had read that Jeff Buckley also used to frequent there. So it was exciting to know that two very diverse scenes had been incubated so close to one another, in fact right across the street from each other.

Each had birthed some notable artists as well; it's the stuff of what some call the "old New York" or maybe just the cyclical nature of things.

So I went on a mission to see what, if anything, I could find out about Regina. I looked her up online, and went and picked up her album *Soviet Kitsch*, Sire 2004, from a record shop in the Village. Once I had an idea what she looked like I don't know if I made a conscious decision, or if it just happened that way, but anytime a girl who remotely resembled Regina would walk by I would say: "Regina?."

I did this, I kid you not, for about a week, and then one day, (It was a Friday or Saturday, I remember it being the weekend) this girl walks by me, and I called out: "Regina," not quite in the form of a question enough so as to feel stupid if it's not her, but with just enough hint of query so as to elicit a positive response if and when applicable. The young woman turns to me and says: "Yes;" not so much as to confirm her identity, rather-more like how I do I know you. When I realized it was really her I couldn't believe it. I couldn't hide how excited I was as I told her about how much I loved her song, "Chemo Limo" and about how my boy Con had put me on to her music, he and one of our other friends Serena, both of whom are big fans; And just as I had done before with Paul Simon, (and Brandon Boyd), I asked Regina if she'd say hello to one of my friends (in this case Con) if I called him. She agreed and I got Con on the phone and was even more excited as she talked to him; so excited that I inadvertently reached back hurriedly for my phone to add just one more tidbit to their conversation, and along with my phone, I pulled her hair.

I was mortified, but she made so light of it, that it blew over real fast-like. She picked up my record and said that she was either on tour or going on tour with The Strokes. I hadn't really talked to any of them at that point, but I told her that they were fans of Pearl Jam as was I. She was so cool and although I haven't seen her since, I met a woman named Wendy who actually does voice training, and works with Regina. Wendy picked up some music from me also, and who knows maybe I'll illicit her voice services one day. It went so well with the whole calling out Regina's name; I decided to try the name-game with others as well.

Now I wish I could say that it took Lucy Liu only a week to show up, but in actuality it took a few months from the time I started calling out her name, to when she finally showed. I had for a long time wanted to meet Lucy. I enjoyed a lot of her work, and I had not too long before then, watched <u>Lucky Number Slevin</u> on DVD, directed by Paul McGuigan, MGM, 2006; plus it don't hurt that she is very easy on the eyes. Josh Hartnett who also starred in that film had picked up my record in Union Square, at the Holiday displays that are erected during the fall.

Anyway, when I saw Lucy, I saw her coming from about a quarter of a block away. I had just enough time to gather myself, clear my throat, and smooth down my shirt. As she walked passed me I offered: "Check out my record." As she took hold of it, I went right into my spiel. She kept walking however as I was describing my music to her. So I finally had to cut my spiel short, and say: "Lucy it's for sale." She glances down at the disc, and then back up at me, and says: "Marvalousss,"still moseying along. So then I said: "Lucy, I'm selling it;" trying to sound firm, and again, she says: "Marvalousss." As the distance between us continued to grow, I then said, with a slight panic in my voice: "Uh, Lucy, you have to buy it." She responded again with the: "Marvalousss" and then she finally disappeared into the drugstore.

I didn't have the heart or the nerve to go in the store after her, or to even wait her out, but I have to say I felt more victorious, than victimized.

Lucy Liu had just taken my album from me, I couldn't have written it any better.

Now here's the kicker; Lucy comes by again a day or two later, and as I'm standing in almost the same spot holding a copy of the same album. I made eye contact with her, and then I said flatly: "Lucy, remember, the album?" Pointing to the one in my hand, she then responds even more matter-of-factly, and flatly: "Oh yeah, I already got that one." I was dumbfounded, what could I say? She was, after all, Lucy Liu.

However if Steve Nash thinks I forgot about that ole, "I don't have my wallet, I was just shooting around down at the park" jazz he gave me in front of Fatbeats that Sunday afternoon, he got another thing coming, who knows, maybe even my new album.

Luke Wilson had also claimed to have no cash on hand once upon an evening, but I told him that I'm a big fan of his and his brother's, and that if and when we saw each other again, I knew he'd be good for it.

Usually when someone says that they don't have the cash on hand, I direct them to any number of ATMs that I pronounce like, (atoms). Which is hilarious to me, because I then go on to tell them that the reason I pronounce them (atoms) is because of the obvious molecular process that allows paper money to appear out of thin air or something like that; I then dismissively tell them that it's really high science and far above my pay grade. Which is usually good for a laugh or two, and I've been known to turn a laugh into some cash every now and again. It's what they used to call laughing all the way to the bank, even if the bank is a sock in your drawer or a slit under your mattress.

One day as a couple of us was heading to the Waverly Diner we noticed an event going on at an establishment that was located right above Grays Papaya. So I innocently just went over to ask the door person what was going on and was told coldly that it was a private affair for a film release. As I walked away, I said in a scoff: "It's not like Philip Seymour Hoffman is in there" and then we made our way across the street to the diner.

No sooner than we sat down in the booth, and looked at the menu, does PHS, walk into the diner. He's joined quickly by a couple, with whom he quickly engages in a conversation. As I sit there trying to decide when and how to make my approach, I somehow figured that coming up from behind him, and tapping him would be a good idea, but it wasn't. He spun around abruptly as if he was startled, but the way he quickly composed himself made me think afterwards that, maybe he had reacted that way to make a point, and he had made it, because at that moment I wished I could've shrunk down and escaped without notice.

Ronald quickly got up from our table and apologized for me and explained to Mr. Hoffman that I had just mentioned his name only minutes before he had walked in.

I recomposed myself, and gave him my album and I mentioned that I went to High School in Greece, N.Y., which is not too far from where he grew up in Fairport, N.Y., both being suburbs of Rochester, N.Y., Our schools even played against each other, and were rivals.

It was cool after that, as I then went on to tell him how hard I laughed while watching him and Laura Linney in that one scene in the film The Savages written and directed by Tamara Jenkins, Fox Searchlight, 2007; which I had viewed at the Angelika Film Center on Houston St.

If you can't tell already, I really enjoy watching movies. Nowadays I find myself more and more interested in those who are behind the scenes as oppose to those who are necessarily in them; and now I have to be more selective about the kinds of movies I watch, and their ratings, because of the whole life, art, and the imitation thereof.

When it comes to films, I now want to know who the producers, directors, writers, and cinematographers are. I even pay attention to who the Best boys and Key Grips are.

It is one thing to respect an actor, but when you learn about the people behind the scenes, and screens who the actors themselves respect you gain a newfound respect for the whole process. The same principle applies to recorded music.

Sometimes actors, like cars are only new and exciting until the next year's model comes along. Sure some hold their value better than others, but most are trying stay on the road for as long as they can keep running.

Cary Grant was quoted by, among others, Charlie Rose during his show on PBS, as saying in response to how long he would continue to act: "Until I can no longer get the girl." After I had finally watched North by Northwest, directed by Alfred Hitchcock MGM, 1959; outside on a drive-in screen, at "Movies Under the Stars" in Cunningham Park last summer in Queens I understood better why he said what he said- some men are just born to play the lead.

I don't know which is harder on the more aged of its performers, Hollywood or the NFL? It must be something to have to look over your shoulder waiting for your replacement to pull up on the lot, or at practice.

On another occasion while I was on my way to pick up my son, I saw Keanu Reeves, at of all places, 14th Street, and Avenue B, not far from the projects. Just as I was about to say something to him, a woman moved determinedly toward him from in front of the Psychic reader booth. I had unsuccessfully tried to get Keanu to stop on the Bowery some months before, and now it seemed I was being eclipsed by this gypsy woman. He seemed so relaxed walking and nodding at each disbelieving passerby who took a second and third glance.

I was trying to call to mind what the name of his band was, and as he was just within earshot of me, the gypsy woman pressed him more urgently, because as she said, she had a special reading for him.

He wanted nothing to do with any reading you could tell, as he emphatically refused, gesturing with his hands to the same effect. I thought it was interesting afterwards that Keanu Reeves, although having been in a band called *Dogstar*, was so adamant about not consulting the stars or however it is they go about fortune telling. From The Matrix franchise alone, he's probably worth a fortune he and The Wachowskis, who directed him, but I digress.

While we're on the subject about discussing the future with celebrities, I stopped Matthew Broderick one day on 6th Avenue, and asked him about a rumor I had heard about there being a sequel to the John Hughes directed, Ferris Bueller's Day Off, Paramount Pictures, 1986. I told him he could pull it off seeing that he looks like he has hardly aged at all. Later that same day I met Steve Buscemi, and told him that I personally owned Trees Lounge, Live Entertainment, 1996, his directorial debut, on VHS. He picked up my record, and threw me some cash, with the caveat: "Don't spend it all in one place." I didn't see Matthew Broderick as often, as I'd see his wife Sarah Jessica Parker walking around the neighborhood. I actually sold a record to one of Matthew's childhood friends, the writer-director Kenneth Lonergan. I mentioned Kenneth to Matthew the next time I ran into him, this time at night and not far from Gray's Papaya.

As we, stood there talking to Matthew, Camreon Diaz walks by, and immediately my attention shifts to her. She stops, and enters our semi-circle and after giving her a quick pitch she enthusiastically agrees to pick up some music from us, and then I realized that Matthew was still standing there, and so I asked him and Cameron if they had ever met. Surprisingly enough, they both nodded to the effect that they hadn't and then made each other's acquaintance right there in front of us, now how cool is that?

That was one of my cooler moments. I've also had my fair share of not so cool moments as well.

Like when although I didn't actually say it to Jeff Beck, I implied by my reference to the "rest of the band;" and by mentioning to him that I had a cool run in with Mick Jagger back in the day, just moments after the revered guitar player had graciously and generously picked up my record. It would seem that I had him mistaken him for Ron Wood. He and Ron Wood resemble each other in my opinion. As my mother would say they favor each other, but I knew from the moment I saw him, that he was a famous rocker, and I even said as I offered him my music: "From one rocker, to another." I just was off by a bit, and minutes later as he headed back in the direction from which he came, probably back to Electric Lady Studios, he seemed a bit perturbed. So I just nodded in appreciation, but afterward I went and looked him up on the internet, and found out he's been in the shadows of other rockers for years, although being a great guitar player in his own right.

It is noteworthy to me that I can find no word or expression to denote un-embarrassing yourself. Even in redeeming oneself you don't undo the effect of the initial embarrassment. You just allow yourself to move above and passed it. Humiliation it seems is right there on the cusp of shame, and not far from the penumbra of guilt. At such a close proximity as can only be measured by light, you just have to shake it off. I don't know what that means exactly I just wrote it to sound smart.

On another day while hustling on 6th Avenue, this time out in front of the IFC Center, which is also one of my favorite theaters. My boy Lil John (not the rapper) works there, and he hooks me up every now and again, and now that I've even gotten acquainted with some of the other staff, (Kasara, Keon, and Ezra) as well, they let me pop in from time to time to see something. This day as I stood in front of the theater however, it was not to watch a film, but people, as they moved by in streams, while I just stood and watched, poised like a Grizzly.

Just then a woman walks by with a wigwam-like patterned shawl on, and a ski hat, wearing spectacles. I offered her my album which she politely declined, and so then I casually said: "From one artist to another;" she looked like an artist, so I said it. The woman walks a few more steps away from me and then turns around and comes back towards me this time reaching for her wallet.

I thanked her for her reconsideration and introduced myself, and asked her name. When she replied: "Patti" I quickly stated, in a moment of discovery: "You're Patti Smith."

I told her what a pleasure it was to meet her, and that I could now scratch her name off my list of people that I wanted to meet. I also told her that I had recently read about her touring with her kids which I thought was cool and she confirmed it.

I wouldn't understand the significance of what prompted her to stop and come back until I watched her interview on PBS with Charlie Rose, not too long after that, maybe just a matter of months. She was talking to Charlie about her new book Just Kids, HarperCollins, 2010, and was relating the story of how she came up with the title. It was while her and her longtime partner, now deceased, Robert Mapplethorpe were walking through Washington Square Park, not far from where her and I had met. They happened on an older couple, and the woman noticing how they were dressed said to the older gentlemen, something like, "Look honey, two artists, take their picture;" and the older man then replied: "They're not artist- they're just kids."

I was blown away to hear her tell that story and then to read parts of her book myself. I understood that it is likely that when I met Patti Smith that day, she possibly had just finished or was putting the finishing touches on her book, and so what I said resonated with her, especially in light of what lay just ahead for her.

"Fire Your Boss"

Producing my own show for several years in NYC, taught me so much. The kind of education you can only get by doing and not by reading or in theory. I learned the least at the times where I thought I knew the most, and I learned much when I recognized that I actually knew little. You can't bank on what people will chose. That's why so many companies spend so much money on R&D. There are so many variables, and invariables that need, and are not likely to be plugged into each varying equation, what was X, last week can be Y, this week and so on.

I recall when VHS and Betamax were in competition while in my teens. I remember some of my friends even having laser disks around the same time. Our family didn't have either initially; in fact we were usually the last family to get any new thing, if ever.

So maybe that is what spurred my interest in which would last, VHS or Beta? I figured even back then that they both basically did the same thing, and so why the two? Eventually VHS went on to thrive, Betamax all but died, and Laser disk morphed into the compact disc which would outlast them all as far as being relevant in the marketplace. Price is always a factor, but the Betamax tape was smaller than the VHS, and by today standards, and leanings people would probably choose Betamax.

When booking artists for shows, what can seem like a no-brainer could end up with you scratching your head. Hip Hop, until recently did not emphasize touring, not like Rock and Country I should say; Now artists are seeing the value of getting out there and touching the audience especially due to the slow demise, and steady decline of record companies, and sales. Ringtones came along as a major source of income and propagated the purchase individual songs, and so naturally albums were constructed with a view to songs, as opposed to a whole composite project. Once you were able to buy one song for about a dollar, especially after the recent phenomenon of many albums only having a few songs that were worth the purchase, it was just a matter of time and arithmetic, before the LP, as we knew it would be affected. Now many artists are putting out EPs not grasping that people will still buy a whole album, if it is indeed, a whole album. Mechanical royalties, aside, the music business has changed dramatically, and that, in my opinion is what has helped to change people's listening and recording habits.

I once finagled my way into Randy Acker's office when he was, unbeknownst to me, part of the top brass at Def Jam. I had met him a night or two before at Foxy Brown's studio session while her brother Pretty Boy was vetting producers. Days after we were at Def Jam for yet another meeting with yet another A&R who had either blew us off, stood us up, or just made us wait. In the interim I asked if Randy Acker was available not aware at all of his position there. I was armed with a cassette not even a cd. Strangely enough he agreed to see me and was tickled about the cassette but heard me spit a verse to the instrumental on the tape anyway. He said he'd liked to hear more but I had not too longed ago gotten to New York, and was ignorant, and so felt I didn't have the connections nor resources to get a song recorded. You must remember this was pre 9-11, back then it was still relatively expensive to record music. Also the guys I knew who had the resources were using them toward what they felt were more promising prospects or just for themselves. I had just transferred to the Saturn dealership in the Bronx, and was worried about paying rent. These are all the factors that would contribute to my DIY ethos; money, bureaucracy, lack of self-confidence, and entitlement. All the same factors that have held so many would be aspirers back from trying to realize their visions. I never went back to Def Jam with my music, and I don't regret it either. No I haven't sold a million records (not yet), or became a household name. I have however worked very hard and gained the respect and even admiration of those whom I respect and admire. It could've very well been that a part of me was even afraid of success, and so I subconsciously sabotaged myself I've seen that happen also.

In April 2003 I was 'Unsigned Hype' in The Source Magazine, which is a distinction, shared by others such as; The Notorious B-I-G, Eminem, DMX, and Common just to name a few. Scram Jones had been featured some months before me, and it would seem that I was on track to signing a record deal, but who knows what really happens behind those doors.

I along with the co-executive producer of my 1st album, Eric "Daytabase" Lee, set up a meeting at one of the majors. The A&R guy, who had also served in the same capacity for a friend of mine, while he was signed to Epic, had us come up to his office. As the music played he just sat there looking uninterested it seemed with the songs, even looking at his two-way pager, and shuffling papers on his desk. He finally stops the music and asked us what we were trying to do, and what was it that he was listening to. The questions took me by surprise, because the answer to both seemed so obvious. I never desired to set foot back into an A&R's office after that. Although I'm not opposed to it, but right then I knew the futility of pushing my vision on people so that they could in turn push their version of my vision on other people. I might as well cut out the middleman and so I did.

Even after my glowing review in The Source, and the fact that we had delivered a finish product, the album still garnered little interest as far as the music industry went. In the years after, I hit the streets with my music, and reaffirmed and confirmed what I had known all along, and that is, that people would like it, even if not everybody, but everything is not for everybody.

Before-I Had to Wait.

Before I hit the streets of New York City to push my music, I worked in the restaurant business for about 5 years. Before that I was a car salesman first in Poughkeepsie, N.Y., and then I transferred to the Bronx. I was from the very start a good salesman, I love people and enjoy conversing with them, and if I must say so myself, I have a pretty good sense of humor. Plus being raised as one of Jehovah's Witnesses, talking to people is what you do in obedience to Jesus' command to: "Go therefore and make disciples of people of all the nations…"; and although I veered or should I say, strayed off the path; the teachings still would overshadow me no matter how far I ran away. So this is somewhat about another prodigal son who also squandered his spiritually rich heritage to go out into the world.

When I first moved to New York with ambitions of making it in the music business, I got fired within the first year of my transfer to Saturn of the Bronx. It's not that I wasn't a good salesman, I was just better at partying; so I would show up to work late, hung over, or worse, not show up at all.

Tom Waits is credited with saying something to the effect that he enjoyed being a rock n roller, because it was the only job that you could come home drunk at 10am, and not worry about getting fired. I think personally, that may have been part of the allure of rock-stardom for me, I have yet to meet Tom, but I did meet Jim Jarmusch on my way to see BRAD, Stone Gossard's other band at The Bowery Ballroom.

Saturn gave me a lot of opportunities. I had been suspended while working in Poughkeepsie a couple of times for being tardy, or absent, but like the music business, the car business is about numbers, and I had them. I found I could push the envelope of what an employer would tolerate, but when the envelope ends up having crystalline powder cocaine in it, my days of being employed, became numbered.

I learned a couple of poignant lesson in the car business. One of my many managers (there is a high incidence of turnover in both the music and car businesses respectively), a guy by the name of Terry told me: "Good deals get better-bad deals get worse."

Mike V another manager I worked under, told me: "Take care of your personal problems- personally" and Carlo would require "Penance" from me when I ran afoul of the work-place rules.

So even before I hit the means streets of New York I learned to hack it, when and where others couldn't, because of having to deal with people who were demanding, condescending, and just plain rude. Handling them with care prepared me in many ways for what I would eventually undertake.

Weeks before my firing in the Bronx I went out on a test drive with two gentlemen interested in this one particular used van, with windows only on the driver and passenger side. I explained that our policy at the store was no test drives on the highway, and that if they wanted to experience highway driving we could use the service road. Once we were in the van though, one of the guys, the test driver took it upon himself to go off the prescribe route and onto the Major Deegan Expressway toward the New York State Thruway.

I felt trapped inside that van with those two hillbillies, but I didn't panic. I calmly instructed the driver to pull over for a second, saying I had heard a suspicious sound, and when we all got out to inspect the vehicle, I got back in real quick like, and left them standing there at the side of the road. About a half an hour later they arrived back at the dealership, and the guy who was driving, came over and poured my own cup of coffee on me. I didn't even get upset, I felt relieved to be back in the dealership and the coffee was lukewarm anyway. One of the service guys, a guy by the name of Lamont couldn't fathom why I didn't react or lash out at the guy. It had been a lesson learned for me, and the lesson was that I didn't want to be in a vulnerable situation like that ever again with strangers, not anywhere, but especially not in New York City. So when they asked me to leave Saturn of the Bronx shortly thereafter, I was ready to go.

Then my boy Rocco who is also from Utica but who I only got to know while living in New York City had heard I was looking for work, so he recommended waiting tables to me. He said it was flexible hours, and good pay, and that a lot of the wait-staff were aspiring people so I'd fit right in. I figured because of my sales and service background it wouldn't be too much of a stretch, and so Rocco put in a word for me at Carmines in The Theater District, where he himself was employed at the time as a waiter.

I started working at Carmines in the height of the theater season. I really liked the buzz of Time Square, especially once I got off work. It was not drab like where I had worked in the Bronx, no matter I didn't last long there at Carmine's either, because although there was a feverish pace, and almost a constant need for servers, they had a zero-tolerance for tardiness.

After my firing, I finagled a job at another restaurant, Mars 2112 which was like working with a bunch of aliens and space cadets, literally. Part of the restaurant's allure was its cosmic theme. I don't remember if I was fired or I just quit, I do remember that I didn't even go to pick up my last check.

After Mars, I ended up at what was then called the WWF aka The World, restaurant, bar, store, and nightclub owned by Vince McMahon and company. They were sued by the World Wide Fund for Nature and ended up changing their name to WWE. Even though I had never been into wrestling, the manager Todd liked that I had worked for Saturn, and so he hired me.

I would watch the eager fans come in for *Monday Night RAW*, and *Friday Night "SmackDown*;" and was bemused at the suspension of disbelieving yet hardcore fans; they even had a championship event called "HardCore" which was a big deal.

While training for the job they had us do what was called "Around the World," which meant that you would work at each position in the restaurant for a shift just so you could better appreciate what the various jobs entailed. The aim was to make each person in every position more sympathetic to the other, so that the various jobs jelled.

Saturn in its inception had interestingly enough, studied the top companies in the world, in whatever their fields were, to see what the methods and contributing factors of their success were. Ergonomics, the study of how people use space comfortably especially in the work place, was one of the contributing factors to the success of many, if not all of the companies.

When we had a little downtime at the restaurant, some of us waiters, and busboys would hang out in the back near the kitchen by the soda machine. For all intents and purposes this was a good place to hang, because if and when a manager would come, you could always act like you were refilling someone's beverage.

Besides the wait staff, there was a then little known aspiring magician who performed his *Mindf*reak show upstairs in the window and around the retail store. He and a woman whom he called his wife would hang in the kitchen as well- his name was Criss Angel.

One day while hanging out by the soda machine with a guy named Brandon, an aspiring wrestler himself, Dwayne "The Rock" Johnson, walks right into the kitchen and up to the both of us at the soda machine and says: "What up;" and as we stood there befuddled, we said nothing, partly out of disbelief, and also because we weren't allowed to talk to the "talent" (as the performers, celebrities, and personalities were called). The venue inside the restaurant had a full stage complete with professional state of the art audio and lights to support concerts, and so we would have performances as well. I remember Lenny Kravitz came to play, and we got word at our shift meeting not to look at him, or to watch him during his sound check. I thought it was ridiculous, but what could I do, I only knew what I had been told, I couldn't do.

I would later meet Lenny at another time and place, and yes even look him directly in his face and give him my music. This was at Joe's Pub, while he was backstage with Chris Rock and Gina Gershon among others. The WWE was an exciting place to work, and I ended up staying there for longer than all the other restaurants I had worked at combined. Which I could have accomplished by only lasting there a month, but I lasted for almost a couple of years.

Ice T would come thru and though I never waited on him personally, I had heard that on one occasion he allegedly ordered a New York strip steak for himself and a kid's meal for his lady friend. What made it even funnier was the fact that the kids meal came in a WWE lunch box at that time, and I must say I liked those lunch boxes; I even had a few of them at home myself. Through the years each time I've ran into Ice T, he seems just as happy to be talking to you as you are to be talking to him.

While working at the WWE or the World, I also waited on Roger Clemmons and his tribe of sons. I was amazed at how many celebrities, athletes and entertainers were into wrestling. One afternoon as I arrived un-customarily early to work, and because the girl who usually handles the refreshments for "talent" wasn't around, I was sent to the "green-room" to deliver a case of bottled water. There was a concert slated that night featuring a band consisting of authors, is what I had been told. I thought nothing of it as I made my way through the corridor in the back, and knocked before entering the room. I walked into the room, and set the water down, all the while, a man stood with his back to me, tuning his guitar. As he shifted to his left I was then able to get a look at his profile and was quite taken aback to see that the man was Stephen King.

Now call it serendipity or whatever, but not even a week before, I had watched his biography on A&E. As I just stood there in the room not saying a word for fear of my job, and at the thought of standing alone in a room (of any color) with the man they call the Master of Horror. I wanted so badly to tell him how inspired I was by his story, at least in part. Having never read any of his books in their entirety, and only having seen a handful of the movies based on them, I never appreciated what a tough time he had before he "made it" so to speak.

Now I've even read that by the time he sold the script for Carrie, and it was slated to be adapted to film, he had all but given up on being a successful writer. He had a young child and despite being distraught, he did the grown-up thing and just took a number of odd jobs. The thing I appreciated was, and still is, is that he had first put in the work, and then in a time he thought it was all but over, his work began to now work for him. His break came, contrary to conventional artistic romanticism, and belief, not because he persevered, but when he had all but given up. Even at that point while standing in the room with Mr. King I had been doing music for long enough, that if music was law, I'd be a lawyer, or medicine, a doctor. I used to think that music owed me something for the suffering I withstood for it. I had decided that I would be content if music would now just work for me, for as long as I had worked for it-some people call that a career.

I regretted not saying anything to Stephen King that day, which I now know help lay the ground for me wanting to fire my bosses. I felt I denied myself what could have been a revealing, and memorable artistic exchange, and for what reason, because I needed my job.

One night while leaving work at the WWE, and heading upstairs through the retail store, and out the door, I saw Mike Tyson standing right there on the sidewalk just feet from me in the heart of Time Square.

As a crowd started to assemble, he then started walking north up Broadway. I also walked along with him flanking him from just off the curb keeping pace, and a respectable distance while yelling: "Yeah Ike," "Yeah Ike;" and each time I would yell it, he would look directly at me, and seem to firm up his shoulder and quicken his pace, as if he was getting amped up. I called him Ike, because during my days in Juvenile hall, two of the boys who were from Brownsville, the very same neighborhood in Brooklyn that Mike is from, told me that "Ike" and not Mike is what they called the boxer around the way, that is to say, the neighborhood. He had already taken the world by storm by then, and we would talk about him often, so what I was told, even back in 1988 seemed like a good little tidbit. Prior to my hiring at WWE, I starting recording my first album; making the commute daily from Washington

Heights to Dayta's house in the Park Slope section of Brooklyn. Dave, one of Dayta's and Scram's schoolmates from Ithaca College, shot the first video off the album for the song "I'm going through it." Some of the film stock we used had even been taken from a Lenny Kravitz's video shoot. One night after our shift was over at the restaurant, I asked one of the sound guys if he could play my video on the huge movie screen with the state of the art sound system. He obliged, and put it on while I, along with the remaining restaurant staff watched it there on the big screen. In that moment, I wasn't even a waiter any more-I was already on my way.

The Advent of September 11, 2001

I was still under the employ of the WWE on the morning of September 11th, 2001. I remember having to work the opening shift at the restaurant which meant I had to be there relatively early. That morning was absolutely gorgeous, with clear sunny skies.

As I prepared for work I vacillated from the bathroom to the room that I rented from an Ecuadorian family in Washington Heights. Someone had left the television on in the living room which was unoccupied at the time. I noticed the reports and live footage of the North Tower on fire and smoke billowing from the skyscraper. At one point the camera nestled in the helicopter showed a panoramic view of Lower Manhattan as viewed from the south. Both the Hudson and East Rivers lay, one on the left, and on the right. The reports were coming in that a plane had crashed, but it wasn't conclusive if it was pilot error or not. After seeing the panoramic view of the island, I doubted very seriously that a pilot given the option of trying to land on the Hudson or East river would opt to fly into a building. This was my reasoning even before Captain "Sully" Sullenberger would successfully land his plane on the Hudson some 8 years later. None of it made any sense to me, but as most did, I went to work anyway.

The trains were still working by the time I headed to work, but inside the subway cars were eerily silent. Once I arrived at work the atmosphere was confused bordering on frantic. I tried to remain upbeat, not because I wasn't deeply affected, but because I was numb. It was obvious to me, that this was, in one way or another, the beginning of the end of the world as we knew it. The Bible describes the time of the end as: "Critical times hard to deal with;" and even though I wasn't regular back at the congregation meetings at the time, I still studied the Scriptures.

In all the confusion, and speculation, I hadn't noticed that Katie wasn't at work that morning, or at least, not at the restaurant.

I had met Katie who was from Indiana along with her roommate Cherese. They were best friends from back home in Indiana, and decided that they would both move to NYC, Cherese first, later to be joined by Katie, and now both were working together at the restaurant.

It was late summer and a group of us decided to go over to the pier one night after work to hang out, drink some beers, and get better acquainted with one another. The Hudson River provided a nice back- drop for the evening, the mood was celebratory; not only were we all working, and moving forward toward our goals, but some, like Katie had already landed a second job. Everything was in flux, and there seemed to be promise in the air. I remember how stoked Katie was about her new job at The World Trade Center. Her excitement was contagious, as was her smile.

It wasn't until after I had been at work for a short while that morning, and saw Cherese, and noticed the worried expression on her face that I even realized that Katie could have been in harm's way, the gravity of the situation then started to sink in. Katie had just started working at the Tower. We all knew that she would have most certainly arrived at work early, but we all tried to stay positive, but it was Tuesday, and the likelihood of having a day off at a new job, that early during the week didn't seem likely. My heart went out to Cherese that day especially. She and Katie were like family, and all the ups and downs that come with that. Katie Marie McCloskey lit up the room when she walked in, and although I didn't know her as well, or as long as I would have liked, I still think about her, and will remember her until we hopefully meet again in God's promised new world.

Where Brooklyn At?

Not long after 9/11 new management came into the WWE, and decided to make some changes, one of those changes, being-me. So I sat back and collected those, what were then, yellow unemployment envelopes which I can say somewhat helped ease the sense of rejection you feel from being fired, especially the week after being recognized for your service.

That's why now, when anyone tells me that they lost their job, I say: "Congratulations" and I mean it. I heard like almost everything else, they have since digitalized unemployment benefits; no matter, I rather get mine from the streets.

The video for my song "I'm going through it" featured an artist by the name of Puerto Rock (Or Jimmy as I know him). We had went to elementary school back in Utica, and he had since moved back to New York City, and secured a record deal with Epic, and was one of the "Whassup" guys" featured in the Budweiser campaigns.

Some of my travels with Puerto Rock are what educated me on much of the downfalls and pitfalls of being signed to a major record company.

I ended up getting another restaurant gig, but this time in Brooklyn, but we'll cross that bridge when we get there.

I first met this guy we called, Locksmith at the *End of the Weak,* the aforementioned open-mike at the Pyramid Club. He was part of a crew called the "Third Eye Navigators". There were a lot of crews back then; I2I, Solid Ground, and our crew, High Society to name a few.

I had mentioned to Locksmith (Anthony) one night that I was in need of a new job, and he intimated to me that his dad owned a restaurant in Brooklyn Heights, and that he'd arranged for me to go by and meet him. He gave me the information, and I remember wondering what kind of restaurant 'Noodle Pudding' might be; I found out it was an Italian restaurant and not Asian like I had presumed. The name comes from, (or so I was told) a loose translation of Anthony and his Father's last name Migliaccio, which is also the name of a dessert on the island of Ischia, located off the coast of Naples, Italy; There the sweet delicacy is known locally as "Noodle Pudding;" and it is where Anthony's father's family is originally from.

Anthony and his father share the same first and last name, but we affectionately called his dad, Anthony Sr., "Toto".

Toto is a man's man, he built much of the restaurant with his own hands, and is there almost every day cooking and greeting guests. Not an educated man by Ivy League standards, but he had one of the highest people IQs of anybody I had ever met. He taught me more about food, wine, and their relationship to people than I had learned at all the other restaurants combined. He knew people, that is, he knew how people wanted to be treated, because he knew how he himself wanted to be treated; which is in itself the basis of a main tenet of Christianity.

Toto was not a religious man per se, but he was big on respect, giving and receiving. We at the restaurant did what we could to avoid his wrath, but sometimes, what could you do?

The restaurant was located on Henry Street, in the shadow of the Brooklyn Bridge. At the time I was still living in Washington Heights, but was accustomed to commuting from Manhattan to Brooklyn being that I did it so often while recording my album with Dayta in Park Slope. One thing that struck me right away about Toto was when he instructed all of us waiters not to introduce ourselves by name when approaching the table. He said that it was an unnecessary gesture, being that we were serving dinner- not invited to it. He added that it allowed us to maintain some of our own dignity, and privacy-I knew right away I liked the guy. A large percentage of the patrons at Noodle Pudding weren't really patrons at all- more like family. I'd say that half were regulars, and by regulars I mean, they ate there weekly. Some ate there multiples times during the week, and at least a handful, visited almost every day.

I really gained a passion for food while working there, and it showed. I remember catching a glimpse of myself in the mirror in the dining room and being amazed at how much my stomach and butt were jutting out in opposite directions. It was sometime around then that I started back with the cocaine. Restaurant people are among the groups of people that really party hard. I had noticed that even back in my days of selling cars in Poughkeepsie, and dealing with some of the folks from the CIA (Culinary Institute of America). I guess because there is such an emphasis on providing others with a good time that some tend to develop some sort of penned up desire for festivity, plus there's a lot of pressure involved as well.

In any event, I started partying again. It didn't help matters when my boy Richie ended up going on an extended vacation to the island of Riker's and asked me if I wanted to sublet his apartment in East Harlem. So I went from a room in Washington Heights, to a one bedroom in East Harlem, and it wasn't long before, I went out of control.

Around the same time I had started recording more frequently with Wicz, Con, Rocco, and Serena in Williamsburg just up the BQE, as my partying got progressively worst. I even started ordering escorts from The Village Voice. It got to the point where it was like ordering a pizza, I'd even ask if any of them came with coke. I'd wait up in the apartment eagerly looking out the window, waiting for the town cars to pull up. Plus on many of my late night rendezvous I encountered, scratch that, I sought out crack heads and dope fiends as well, yeah I know-disgusting. I caught an infection in my eye, which exacerbated my already problematic skin, and I was appalling to look at for a time.

Finally Toto called me in the restaurant bathroom, handed me an envelope, and said simply without any hint of emotion: "Don't come back."

I'm so thankful to Jehovah God that I never contracted AIDS, especially since it had seemed that I was trying extra hard to get it. It was a toxic and unhealthy lifestyle and I was trapped in it. Like so many Japanese tourists I've watched compulsively sucking in cigarette smoke outside of jazz clubs, no longer even seeming to get the least bit of pleasure from smoking-just damaging themselves, because damaging one's self has become the addiction.

I thought maybe all my self-destructive behavior was due to me trying to punish myself for all the dirt I did, especially back home in Utica.

While working at Noodle Pudding I waited on the likes of the aforementioned Gina Gershon; Paul Giamatti, famed attorney Barry Sheck, and Melina Kanakaredes.

I remember one night Ms. Kanakaredes came into the restaurant with her family, and sat at the table that was adjacent to the espresso machine, and one of my fellow waiters, who also tended bar at times, and was an aspiring actor himself, kept doing impressions, and weak impersonations of, like the Marx Brothers, all because she was within an earshot.

I felt bad for him; in fact I was embarrassed for him at the time. I'm sure he didn't care though, and felt more embarrassed for me for my drug and whore habit which I neither hid nor publicized, necessarily, but had become the thing of restaurant legend.

Working at a restaurant and making good money makes it hard to be hungry (pun intended) in a creative sense. People get complacent, and their drive wanes. The job truly becomes the "gig" as we often call it, no longer aspiring for anything further.

During my few years at Noodle Pudding, the great Northeast Blackout of 2003 occurred, and on that day, against Toto wishes, I opted to go home. Some of the waiters and busboys especially were very nonchalant about it.

During my time in the restaurant business in general I had heard hearsay from some of the guys from Mexico about individuals having to pay the "Coyote;" in other words the point man at the border crossings whose job it is to find and assure safe passage across the border.

So even though we all needed money, some needed it more desperately than others, and maybe that's why many of them decided to stay.

With 9/11, still fresh in my mind I had recalled hearing stories of the employees who were told by their employers in the second Tower to: "Go back to work"; so they stayed at work, for fear of losing their jobs.

So once again I was out of a job, but still in Richie's apartment, the same apartment where he and I had spent countless hours smoking, and listening to all kinds of music; Paul McCartney, Paul Simon, Donovan, and Elvis Costello. I would eventually meet them all, but at that time I had another big problem, my appearance, I looked like the Creature from the Black Lagoon, directed by Jack Arnold, Universal International, 1954. There was no restaurant, or any place of business, I imagined, that would hire me looking the way I did.

I remember one Sunday morning shortly after being let go from Noodle Pudding I was at this eatery called "Pan-Pan" that used to be located on 135th Street & Lenox Avenue in Harlem. Joe Budden was also there, he was at that time in regular rotation on the radio, and abuzz in the streets. I mustered up enough nerve, despite my appearance, to approach him and ask for his contact information if I could. I figured I might as well try to get back on my music grind since I wasn't waiting tables. I'll never forget the look on his face when he turned and saw me. It was a look of utter and restrained disgust. I should apologize to Joe if I made him lose his appetite that morning, he should know that I was just trying to salvage the little bit of self-respect I had left. I understood though, when it comes to business, presentation is so important. After some time, as my face started to reappear, and as the cash in that envelope Toto had given me, started to disappear I realized that I again needed to start looking for work.

This time I turned to another fellow emcee, LEFTist was his name, and I knew him from both the *End of the Weak*, and *Freestyle Mondays* which was another open-mic hosted by a guy named Ill Spoken, accompanied by Mariella, Cuzme, Dave, and Claudio et al. Years earlier, I sat in with the band that would eventually make up Freestyle Mondays, along with a singer whose name was Eddie. Just to give a little historical background, because both movements have since gone worldwide, and I just happened to be there at the inception of both.

So LEFTist was part of a crew called "Mindspray" along with this kid called Dyalekt, and another emcee named "C.O.N.C.E.P.T" that I was cool with. LEFTist also worked at a restaurant called "Luna Park" that was located in the rear of Union Square Park in Manhattan. He hooked me up with an interview and I got the job. It was an outdoor place, and because I was a new hire, they told me that I would have to start off with the morning shift, which meant that I would be making almost nothing as far as tips. So, at around the same time I started heading over to the record store Fat Beats, after my shift ended in the afternoon.

I had run into Creature at the Bowery Ballroom down on Bowery & Delancey Street, and that same night he saw me just give my record to Jean Grae, another emcee and artist I had met, coming up on the scene. I remembered meeting Jean some years earlier when Scram Jones and I went to the Chelsea Hotel to meet with her. I didn't' say much then, but it tickles me to think that I not only met Jean Grae, the rapper, but would also meet Famke Janssen who plays Jean Grey on film, and both ended up with my music. Anyways I gave Jean Grae my album outside the club and upon greeting Creature moments later he asked me: "What'd you do that for?" In response to seeing me just give her my music for free. I replied cavalierly: "Oh I have boxes at home" and I did. He shook his head, still in disapproval, and said that I should bring some of those CDs out to Fat Beats.

Now here's what I find so remarkable. I had first met Creature while I was living in Poughkeepsie, and traveling back and forth to visit my son, and before he was born, his mother. On one of those trips, as I'm walking through the aisle on the Metro North train, I happened upon this dreadlocked dude writing in his notebook. I could tell by his almost inaudible grunts that he was reciting lyrics. I asked if he was am emcee, and a conversation ensued. His gruff voice and gritty passion made an impression on me right away, plus who could forget a guy named

Creature? We rode the rest of the way down to NYC, and once we arrived we bid each other farewell, and went our separate ways. The next time I would see him would be years later, at Fat Beats, and then at the Bowery Ballroom. So it had been a few years since our initial meeting on the train heading to New York from upstate. I think it interesting that I initiated a conversation about music, with the very guy who would show me how to initiate conversations about music, and transition those conversations into cash transactions.

So I was making almost no money at Luna Park there in back of Union Square Park, and my rent was backed up. I would sit on the futon in Richie's apartment that I was still supposed to be subletting, with my head in my hands wondering how I could make some money. It turns out that I was actually sitting on the answer. Under the futon lay several boxes of unopened CDs of my album The Wonder Years. I remembered what Creature had said, and I figured, why not give it a shot, I had nothing to lose.

On September 18th, 2006, LEFTist was killed, in a hit-and-run accident on the West Side Highway. I never thanked him enough for the opportunity he afforded me, or explained to him my reasons for wanting to move on. I look forward though to welcoming him, Joshua D. Crouch, and others back in the promised resurrection.

It would be a Saturday morning that I would finally take the plunge from being a waiter, to becoming a hustler. I had been out late Friday night knowing that I was scheduled to work the opening shift at Luna Park the next morning. I had went out to hustle along with the guys over the course of the past week, and had done better out in the street than I was doing per shift at the restaurant when comparing my daily earnings to my nightly ones.

My phone rang that Saturday morning and I cracked one eye open to look at the number, and once it stopped ringing I received a voicemail notification. So I woke up just enough to retrieve and listen to the message. It was my manager, a woman named Kim. She basically said that I knew I was on the schedule to work that morning, and if I didn't show up, I would no longer have a job. I remember my first thought being that your employer is not supposed to fire you over the phone, and my second was that I had a choice, and so I chose to lay back down, and go back to sleep, because I knew I would never fire myself.

At first I was nervous at the thought of not having anything else to fall back on. In fact that nervousness would stick around for about the next

18 months. I remember when it finally subsided. It happened on 23rd Street. For no discernible reason I just thought to myself: "I can do this;" and I felt a calm come over me, and as I exhaled the anxiety dissipated.

The rest of the guys who I stood along with all seemed so contented, and so many of the people we talked to, going to and fro to work, seemed so miserable; I had an epiphany one evening while walking in Alphabet City. I walked past a restaurant on Avenue A with a nice décor, and there was a server, a woman leaning against the bar of an empty restaurant. It occurred to me that people put their livelihood in the hands of others, and that's well and good, except someone has to do the groundwork. So there she was leaning, hoping, and waiting for a customer to come through the door. If the owner and management did their job, it would be an eventful day for her. Somehow some way, someone had to attract customers, and there was no shame in it on any level. Plus everyone knows a good server doesn't lean in plain sight.

One of the first things you learn when selling anything are the selling points. Product knowledge is the key, and who knew more about my musical product than me?

Personality goes a long way as well, because, again, you're actually selling yourself. Another hurdle to get over is the discomfort with talking about money, working at Saturn taught me that the more value that you build in your product, the more confidently you can broach the subject of payment. Another point to consider, are the FOOs (Frequently Offered Objections). In the car business we had "Ups" or turns to determine which sales consultant are next in the rotation to speak to a guest when people would come in the door, or onto the lot.

As a waiter it was at times, according to the seating, which server would get the next table, or if you pooled your tips it really wouldn't matter, because the tips would ideally be distributed equally.

In the streets it was more of a free-for-all, although there was etiquette, some unwritten rules that we followed. It was frowned on to interrupt the conversation of another hustler while they were talking to a potential supporter. It was a delicate balance though, between not interrupting, and making your presence felt before the person walked away without seeming intrusive.

If someone picked up AB Do Well's record for instance, and I waited too long to segue into my spiel, it could be over once they started off on their way. However if during his conversation I stood at a respectable distance, and even greeted the person in acknowledgement, it would allow me to transition to my music in a seemingly more seamless fashion. As long as someone worked within our system we made it easier by even making a brief introduction in their behalf, before continuing on with our pitch. However if someone was a loose cannon and didn't comply with the unwritten rules, they wouldn't last because our system was so smooth that any different approach seemed abrasive and out of place. The best business models are adaptable; if it comes down to cost then if the cost doesn't come down, the value must then come up.

This you are now reading is indicative of what I just wrote. Selling CDs was becoming increasingly harder, and the prospect of repackaging, rehashing and returning to selling CDs, after recording new music wasn't cost effective or practical; plus technology is moving further and further away-the way technology does. More and more the people that I encountered didn't even have disc drives on their laptops, or even use CD players for that matter. I didn't have a robust R&D department at my disposal. So all I needed was to look at what the big companies were doing to see what I needed to do. If they've stopped making a product, it's probably because to some extent people have stopped buying it. My business model had to change.

A book however is a whole other story. You don't need studio time or musicians for that matter. No modern technology is even required, and even blind people have Braille available to them. I venture to say that no matter how popular e-books become they still won't replace actual books in the way that mp3s replaced the physical copy of an album in its various formats. After all you can't impress people who come to your home with how well read you are the same way, with a tablet. Like movies and books, our lives are replete with foreshadows, flashbacks, ironies, and symbolisms that manifest at times without leaving a hint of their significance until the moment has already passed. Time, after all is the largest involuntary muscle.

The Utican

I feel it rude to go on without telling you a little more about myself. My name is Marcus Xavier Taylor, and I was born in Utica, New York. Which is situated about 239 miles Northwest of NYC which, when I was growing up seemed like a thousand miles away; in that not many people that I knew made the trip too often, and the few who did were welcomed back as if returning from an exotic faraway land.

Some of us from Utica like to highlight the fact that Utica is not, upstate, but rather Central New York. New York City is after all, arguably, the most famous city in the world and being known in NYC, is like being known by one of the world's biggest celebrities; cities, like people themselves yearn to be put on the map, often driven by a presence inside them desiring to be better than its former incarnation.

Like a city with an older more popular sibling, Utica has always had a desire to establish its own identity, and not in its relation to NYC.

I have four sisters: Ramona, Valora, Jerri, and Tamara, and I am the only man child. Ramona was raised in Dothan, Alabama, and Valora spent much of her formative years in Providence, R.I., both living with extended family, leaving me the only boy still with two sisters in the house, plus my mother Bobbinell, and my father Jeremiah.

My father became one of Jehovah's Witnesses when I was just a toddler. Interestingly enough, it was my mother who first agreed to study with the Witnesses, and my father would try to avoid them; even at least on one occasion jumping out of the back window, as my mother tells it.

My father said that he had always been searching for God, and indignant at the injustices in the world. Our storied pasts, my father's and mine, somewhat resemble each other like our features do. Drugs, hustlers, women, and violence had a corrupting influence on the both of us; my father unlike me however never went to prison.

My father's family is from Summerton, South Carolina; he had ten other siblings, and my mother with seven siblings, was born and raised in Dothan, Alabama.

My father's father, my grandfather was a deacon in the church and my grandmother, my father's mother, was also very active and highly regarded in the Pentecostal church as well; even becoming a deacon herself if memory serves.

My grandfather organized bus groups, and trips to go work the beaneries in the surrounding areas just outside Utica. It may have been the beaneries that brought my mother's side of the family up to Utica as well.

My mother's aunt Mildred who they called "Sister Gal" had come to Utica to work, but had gotten into a skirmish, and so my mother's grandmother sent my mother to see about her aunt. That's how my mom ended up in Utica.

My mother ended up living close to my father's family, and so befriended some of my father's sisters, my aunts. The rest is, well, part history, and part biology.

My father's oldest brother, my uncle, who was then named Lawrence, upon my birth, named me after Marcus Garvey- the famous Black Nationalist, and Malcolm X, the Islamic leader, and Civil Rights activist. My uncles and aunts were very socially and politically active in the community. I even hear that Jesse Jackson was at one time a friend of the family. My uncle would later change his name to Amefika to embrace his, and by relation, our African ancestry. He even traveled back to Africa, and related to us that our ancestors were originally from Sierra Leone, and that the ship and slave-masters felt that, due to the similarity in the topography of South Carolina, to parts of the coast of West Africa, that the enslaved wouldn't be as restless.

I mentioned what my uncle had told me, when I recently met Henry Louis "Skip" Gates Jr. This after his specials on race and genealogy started airing on PBS. He neither confirmed nor denied it.

Professor Gates, you may remember, after the infamous mistaken home-owner-identity debacle, saw the rise of some of the same questions on race, and his own public profile; this all before I gave him my record.

My father said he started getting serious about God when he began studying the Bible, examining his life and desiring the best for his family. He was baptized as one of Jehovah's Witnesses soon after and as long as I can remember has sought to serve God.

My mother has yet to be baptized as one of Jehovah's Witnesses, but she still studies from time to time. Religion would have a polarizing effect on my family as Jesus himself foretold, that people would be divided over him, and naturally so because he said there was only one road leading off into life, and it "cramped "and that "few are finding it."

My parents would divorce, re-marry, and divorce again, and because we didn't celebrate the pagan holidays we were somewhat estranged from both my father's, and my mother's side of the family. Distance would also play a part as well. Although during the holidays we would use those occasions to visit my father's side of the family in Utica, being that most of my mother's immediate side of the family lived in Providence and in the South, we didn't get to visit them as often as we liked.

When my parents split the first time we moved to Providence for a time. It was during that time that I witnessed my first killing. It was our neighbor, a man, I only remember as "Joe;" and it was at the hands of his own wife, who when I walked out into the hallway and looked up the stairs, and seen the grisly scene of him, with a butcher knife sticking out of his chest, seemed to just smirk, and then she just walked casually back into the apartment that they shared.

We had hamburgers for dinner that night, and I remember not wanting to eat the burger, because the ketchup reminded me of the blood that ran down Joe's chest.

My mother's brother, my uncle Paul, or Carl as we call him, was her only sibling who lived in Utica, so we would visit him and his family regularly.

My uncle loved guns, and so did my mother's father, my grandfather, though not related to my uncle. I spent much of my early childhood playing; spending time with my dad, going fishing, making repairs and going to Bible study at the Kingdom Hall.

I even help build some of the meeting places and attended conventions as far away as Canada. My father even brought me to the World Headquarters of Jehovah's Witnesses in Brooklyn, New York, when I was approaching puberty; but as my parents' relationship started to deteriorate, I started hanging out with the wrong crowd. Like the Scripture says: "Bad associations spoils useful habits." That's how it started with me.

I sought out bad associates, and then eventually became one. Being the only boy growing up, I felt the need to learn to defend myself. It wasn't until I came to New York that I witnessed people regularly yelling at one another, even at the top of their voices, and then going their separate ways without further incident. In Utica there would usually be violence that followed.

I enjoyed watching and reading about Bruce Lee and martial arts in general like many of my generation, which in itself was and is still a departure from the teachings of Jesus Christ. I started drinking first, and then smoking weed to start, but I wasn't finished.

My father and mother eventually separated, and he decided to move to Rochester, New York. He sat us 3, my sisters Jerri and Tammy, and I down at the dinner table, and informed us of his decision to move, and gave us a choice to stay with my mother or to leave with him.

My older sister Jerri and I opted to stay in Utica with my mom. I don't know what Jerri's motivation was, but mine was freedom- being that my father was the disciplinarian of the family. Tammy ended up in Rochester with my dad.

During my parents time together my mother was quiet most of the time, until she started drinking. That's when she'd put on some Millie Jackson, and act up. It would be unfair to say that it was only my mom's drinking that caused my parents to split, even now, as I'm still trying to understand what it was that caused my mom to drink.

My sister Ramona, her oldest, but by a different father, was basically kidnapped by my mother's father, my grandfather, this many years ago. It is even said that my grandmother, my mother's mother though never married to my grandfather, assisted in the removal of my sister from the home, it sounds complicated I know.

So I knew there was pain both latent, and apparent. My mother had a knack for printing and photography. Looking back now I can better appreciate her need for expression. She even went back to school and earned an Associate's degree.

I remember how pleased my mom seemed with a camera in her hand, and how passionate she would describe the processes of printing, and film development but I couldn't at the time fully appreciate her passion.

My father had a lovely voice, and would sing in the house, and in the car, and at Bible study. He was very handy as well, and I thought, as kids often do, that there was nothing my father couldn't do.

Before he left for Rochester he drove the city bus in Utica. I remember he'd forbid us on some days to go to a city pool called Addison Miller which was located on the other side of town in west Utica.

In order to get there we had to cross Genesee St. which was where his route took him. Not being familiar with bus schedules we'd cross that street sometimes with sheer determination, like gazelles crossing a water hole in the Serengeti. We figured like those hapless deer that we had probability on our side. We'd dart out toward the busy street and every so often just as we made, or were about to make it to the other side, my father's bus would drive by us and he'd see us in plain sight and we him, wagging his finger. We figured since we were caught anyways, we might as well go ahead and take the swim.

My sister Valora, before she left for Providence, would sneak out of the house to go to house parties; I remember going with her to this one run-downed club called the, "Black Crystal". She being several years my senior, I looked up to her, and would sneak out to follow her. She was also one of the first Poppers in Utica, when Break dancing and Pop Locking became popular. She was part of a crew called UNI-TRICITY.

Hip Hop or Rap as we called it, was already taking the world by storm, and a local DJ (Big B) would play breaks and classics at those parties and I would just stand around, on the wall mostly, being that I was noticeably younger and not of drinking age, and way too self-conscious to try to dance.

So I just stood there taking it all in. Mark Brooks aka Mark G, was the foremost emcee, and would rock on the mic surrounded by the likes of Jay Zak, Count Mix-Down, and City Kid. Those were some of our Cold Crush brothers, our pioneers, our grand and mix-masters in Utica.

I always gravitated to the guy on the microphone, as he'd talk playfully over the beat break, and call for calls and responses, and get them. He usually had a drink in his hand and a girl not too far from his side. That's who I wanted to be. It required no technical knowledge or equipment on my part, plus nobody was cooler than the MC. Another one of the older guys that I noticed on the scene even before then, was a guy named Robert Garrett, who, once the Five-Percent Nation's teachings finally made it to Utica, and in homage to the legendary Emcee of the same name, would become known as Rakim.

Rakim or Rob as we knew him first didn't rap, or Dee Jay, but he was just as popular as the guys that did. He was intimidating but he had charisma, and even had somewhat of a following himself; to help him with his coat and what not.

By the time my father moved away to Rochester, I immediately stopped attending Bible study at the Kingdom Hall, and even school for that matter. I started getting into mischief, and one of the older guys from the neighborhood encouraged me to get it all out of my system, before I could be charged as an adult. It seemed like a logical idea at the time except it presupposed that I would eventually get caught, and treated like an adult. So me and a few buddies set out to see just what we could get away with.

My mother, seeing that I was getting out of control, and because she probably missed him, would call my father who would come down to Utica from Rochester from time to time to try and take me back with him; just to have me escape from the house as he entered, and even once from inside of his car.

On one occasion he jacked me up so hard by my collar that my legs almost dangled off the ground. I couldn't even talk, not even to warn him that my mother was coming from behind him with a 2x4 with his name on it, and with one whack to his shoulder I was off again.

Robert had a nephew named George who was around my age, and who was someone who I really looked up to. He was the best emcee of our generation, and could freestyle for days with a delivery like none I had heard before. We listened to all the classics, Rap, Rock, and because it was the 80's, Pop, whatever sounded good.

We would congregate at Utica Free Academy, the local high school, during the basketball games, and entertain ourselves and others not even watching much of the games. We'd have impromptu rap battles at a place called Johnson Park on top of a large circular water fountain that would double as our stage. We quadrant off areas of the neighborhood and rename them according to the Boroughs. My neighborhood (Cornhill) was the Bronx aka Pilon. My MC name was at first Casanova, then Mark Manhattan, and before long I settled on Craze. Deon one of my partners was called D-Brooklyn. As you can see, we had already in our imaginations, transported ourselves to NYC.

As it happened I along with a group of friends started burglarizing stores; first a sneaker store-which we then cleaned out. We had enough sneakers and Starter jackets to last for weeks and weeks. Then we hit a jewelry store, and after crawling around on the floor for some time I noticed a red beam on my wrist, and realized that we had tripped the alarm. By the time we looked up the police were already outside. So we agreed that we'd hold up in the store, that is until we heard them radio in for the dog. We were arrested and because of our ages, we were released to our parents pending our court dates.

No sooner than we hit the streets, this time, I along with a few more buddies was back at it again. We hit a gun store, and this time got away with about 10,000 dollars' worth of handguns. I personally had almost every caliber of handgun. When we had robbed the sneaker store, one by one the neighborhood tough guys would show up at our (usually my) house; and to keep the peace we would appease them with a jacket or a pair of sneakers. When the word got out that we had hit the gun store, there were no more visits; we were armed & dangerous.

One night we came upon a group of revelers at the Utica Parkway, who had made a bonfire using the inside of an oil drum. We asked if we could join them, and they readily agreed warmly welcoming us. I noticed another oil drum off in the distance, and pointing to it I asked if they minded if we "made a little noise?" They assured us that they wouldn't, and as we walked toward the oil drum they even rooted us on, not realizing it would be the noise of semi-automatic weapons. Everyone ran for cover. A few days later, and after one of the other guys pistol whipped another guy from the neighborhood, I woke up with detectives hovered over me. I went for another ride downtown, and this time I wouldn't be coming right back home. They held three of us at a juvenile facility until our court dates, and then we were promptly given 18 months, the maximum time a juvenile could receive. I went to a place called Annsville located in Oneida County, New York. One of the other two went to a place called Industry near Rochester, New York, and the other dude went to Tryon, not far from Albany, N.Y., the same facility where Mike Tyson had been released from just some years earlier.

The day before we were shipped from the detention center I decided to cross the line of the mess hall to the girl's side to kiss a curly blond headed girl I had been making eyes with over the course of days. Although the facility was co-ed, we rarely saw the girls except at chow. I made my way over to her, under penalty of; I didn't know exactly what the penalty would be, and I didn't care I was leaving the next day. So I placed my hand on her shoulder, ever the hopeless romantic, and bent around to kiss her. She laughed then met my lips with hers, and the reason she laughed became apparent when remnants of scrambled eggs filled my mouth. It was still a memorable kiss, and I still like eggs till this day.

Annville Youth Camp was a rude awakening. Unlike the detention center it had elements of military school, and an emphasis on discipline that sometimes went beyond corporeal punishment. It was not unusual to see boys with "rug burns". It was miserable at first for most of the new boys, then once we got used to the program it became easier. There were lots of boys from NYC; in fact I'd say that the majority were from the Boroughs. I met kids from Brooklyn, Queens, The Bronx, and Manhattan. Many had come from Spofford, a detention facility where they sent juvenile offenders from New York City, and the surrounding areas; which from my understanding was somewhat of what they called a gladiator school.

This all, at the time I should have been entering my second year of high school; instead I was entering a world that would ultimately condition me for entry into another world to come.

There was a huge emphasis also on sports and athleticism. We attended school and shop classes during the day, and worked out in the gym and played sports during recreation, and on the weekend.

Our shop teacher was a man named Mr. Abbis who happened to be a black belt in Judo. He was a mild tempered man with a great sense of humor; and no one gave Mr. Abbis a problem. He could rip a phone book in half with his bare hands and every so often he would demonstrate it in class-it never got old. Annsville was divided into 5 teams as they were called. Each team was assigned a number and color; I was in Team 4 which was Blue if memory serves. We had a large dormitory that was sectioned off into 5 sections each with beds, all of which were covered in sheets and bedding of the same color that corresponded with the color of each team. So as you walked into the dorm and along the corridor you'd walk by teams: 1, 2, 3, 4, &5.

There were staff assigned to each particular team and although they sometimes fluctuated from team to team, they would stick to one team for the most part.

Our Staffs were Mr. Pugh, an old military retiree who worked in the mornings. He was a sweet man, grandfatherly in his approach but his Navy background also made him very pragmatic. Mr. Pugh also had a younger relative that also worked with us; he was a cool guy, a body-builder who had an easy way about himself as well. There was Mr.

Brown who was a former football player, and athlete, and still had the physique to show it. Mr. Brown didn't take any shorts; he was quick-tempered, but there was also an avuncular quality about him. I remember one afternoon he called us all in to the office,(each individual team had an office where the boys would have group sessions, do school work and watch television).

Mr. Brown had brought in a movie; and he put in the VHS tape as he commented to us about us thinking we were tough (he was part of the reason why).

The film was The Color Purple, directed by Steven Spielberg, Warner Bros, 1985. Based on the novel written by Alice Walker, and we all watched in silence. After the film was over, Mr. Brown turned the lights back on, and all you could hear was sniffling and the whining tearful complaints of how, "stupid that movie was." I would meet Whoopi Goldberg 20 years later in SoHo, but I didn't think at the time of telling her that story. I approached her as she moved toward a waiting van, but she kindly stopped long enough to accept my album and accolades.

Another Staff was Kenneth Pollard (or Pub) as we called him back home. I knew Pub from back in Utica; he had nephews around my age, who even back then was involved in Rap music.

Pub was also a highly regarded Martial Artist, and at night while the other boys lay in their beds, Pub would call me up to the front, and I'd sit on the floor next to his chair that faced our team section in the dorm. Each section had a chair so that the staff could sit and watch us as we slept, and each team consisted of between 8 and 14 boys.

Pub would tell me about things happening back in Utica, and encourage me to finish the program and get out of there. Other boys would be called up to sit down as well.

We had levels that allowed certain privileges too. Once you reached a higher level you could even go to the movies, and other activities outside the facility, and into the nearby towns, and cities, one of which was my city Utica, N.Y.

Another movie they brought in for us to watch on VHS was Bull Durham, directed by Ron Shelton, Orion Pictures, 1988; and starring among others, Kevin Costner, Susan Sarandon, and Tim Robbins.

I never understood why they would bring a movie like that for a bunch of adolescent boys to watch in the mountains. I instantly became a fan of the three stars. Especially Susan Sarandon and Tim Robbins who I hadn't remember seeing on screen before. How could I know back then that they would not only become a couple, but also a couple of supporters of my music?

I made my next level and was slated to go to the Uptown Theatre in Utica to watch a movie with the group. The movie selected was <u>Permanent Record</u>, directed by Marisa Silver, Paramount Pictures, 1988. Starring a then little known actor named Keanu Reeves, about a high school student who commits suicide. It was a very touching film during a very emotional time, because I felt as if I was also throwing my life away.

So understand that I'm not just name-dropping for the sake of name-dropping, but with an aim of picking up the pieces. The Uptown Theatre was also the very first 70mm theater in Utica, N.Y.

As my mother tells it, on the eve of giving birth to me, she along with some friends, snuck in to see James Brown at the Utica Auditorium. So I think it fitting that the first concert I attended was to hear the man they called "The Godfather of Soul," and "The hardest working man in show business;" and that it was through the back door. Right before giving birth to my sister Jerri, who is 14 months my senior, my mother went to see The Dells, at the Apollo Theater in Harlem. She said nothing about sneaking in on the latter occasion, but either way I think that those kinds of prenatal excursions informed both my sisters' and I take on music and attitude, that music is for the taking. My first official concert was to see Public Enemy, The Beastie Boys, and Murphy's Law, in Syracuse, N.Y., while on the lam. Years later while visiting Vazac's Horseshoe bar on 7th Street and Avenue B, to see where they filmed some of The Godfather II. As I walked passed the bar I overheard a guy, in response to a song that had just started to play over the speaker say that: "Back when we opened for Metallica in Belgium." Just that fragment of his anecdote was enough to peak my interest, and so I backtracked two steps, and said: "Whoa you were in a band that opened for Metallica?" The tone in my voice challenging yet innocently cynical enough to mask my obvious eavesdropping; The guy turned out to be Jimmy Gestapo, and to call him the lead singer of Murphy's Law would be a disservice, so I'll just say the voice behind, or in front of Murphy's Law. I told Mr. Gestapo about my buddies and mine, trip to Syracuse, and about his band being my first concert, and some of the circumstances surrounding that weekend back in the Eighties. Murphy's Law along with Bad Brains was two of my first tastes of Hardcore music, and interestingly enough, before CBGB's closed, Bad Brains was invited to play, and fittingly so, as the last Hardcore show. I showed up not having the $50 for the ticket that night, and ended up jumping the fence, and going through the back door with, Creature, John Joseph of the Cro-Mags, and Darryl Jenifer of Bad Brains.

"The Utican Part II"

The young men in Annsville were all there on an assortment of crimes; some more serious than others. No one really spoke about what they were "in for," but you could sometimes sense who were of the more serious offenders.

The facility consisted of a school area, cafeteria, gymnasium, and dormitory. We competed against the other teams, ate with the other teams, and ultimately we became a family.

One of the kids, who arrived at the facility and was placed in my team, was a young man from the Binghamton, N.Y., area. He was probably the first real 'head-banger' I had come to know, and to my surprise I found him to be an intelligent, sensitive, and courageous individual, who just happened to be white, in a facility where, as you might imagine-he was the minority.

Yet he held his own, never backing down, even in the face of some of the more abrasive and rugged kids from New York City. He would also have the dubious distinction, years later, of being one of the first people in New York State's history to receive a homicide conviction based on DNA evidence.

I would eventually leave Annsville upon completing my sentence, but not to go back to Utica, at least not for a while. I ended up back with my father in Rochester, which before long started to feel like a whole other detention facility. Things were well enough to begin with, I enrolled in high school, and even got a job washing pans at a bakery. My father even got me a car, which at the time I scoffed at.

It was an early model Plymouth or something like that. It was big, green, and ugly, and I didn't like it, which probably had more to do more with what I thought my peers would think, because I know that now I would really appreciate having that car.

I had a similar experience with my son recently, with a baseball cap. I gave him a vintage Atlanta Braves cap with the old stitching, but he didn't want it simply because it's not what the other kids were wearing. I recall while we were working at Noodle Pudding, Toto telling his son Anthony: "That style is sometimes not having any style."

I had started attending the Kingdom Hall again with my father, but before long, my association, and rebelliousness, would again rear their ugly heads.

I started writing lyrics at the same time, which for me was a new experience, because for most of my early years rapping, I had free-styled, which is to say I rhymed words and sentences extemporaneously off the top of my head- as we all did in the beginning.

I started running away from my father's house before long and breaking into cars. My father would make unannounced visits to my high-school, to search my locker, and just thinking about it now makes me hope that I never have to experience the stress of having a child that is so out of control.

He also took the television out of the house; referring to it as the "idiot box," and although I resented him for it then, I often times throughout my life, and even now as I write this-do not have a television at my immediate disposal.

I recall this one particular incident with my father and the television. It happened during one of the rare times that, we as a family had cable. As my father was flipping through the channels, it landed on a channel with a man and woman in the deep throes of passion. He was distracted, and so didn't realize what was on the screen, but I wasn't and had. Once he got wind of it, he quickly turned the channel, but the images remained with me, and so I grabbed the T.V. guide (ask somebody) flipped through the pages, and found the title of the film, hoping maybe to resume my viewing at a later date. I was in my teens, and that later date wouldn't arrive until I was almost 40 years old. The movie, though good, would not prove to be what I thought it was back then, but the book as you might expect was even better.

Although I was enrolled in high school and exhibited an aptitude for learning, and sports, I never really excelled at either. Coach Drum, the school's basketball coach, who saw potential in me, and possibly the direction I was headed in, even offered to have me come and live with him, even though it would mean I'd play with his son, but on an opposing team. Part of my problem was I never really applied myself as my father would say.

We lived in Greece, N.Y., which, again, is a suburb of Rochester. I started hanging out with this kid, who also seemed to have a knack for trouble; we'll call him "White-boy Dave." It was Dave who introduced me to smoking freebase cocaine.

To constitute smoking Crack, back then you had to have added components like, I think ammonia, that slightly differed from just heating and then cooling cocaine and baking soda before smoking it, but it was all the same idea. The first hit I took off the pipe made my ears ring. I never forgot that ringing either. One day Dave and I went into the city of Rochester. We ended up in this, what could only be described as a crack den, and after spending a considerable amount of time there, I remember looking around the room, and seeing ages that ranged from early teens to seniors. It was sad, but I still didn't want to leave, hoping for just another crumb to smoke. I also hung out with a kid name Brian who drove a red Hyundai which he had gotten when the car company was still fairly new. Hyundai has not only survived, to maybe the surprise of many, me included, but it has thrived.

Bryan was cool; we played basketball, and hit the weights afterschool. We would crash some of the school parties in town and in the area, and usually end up in fights, but we didn't care we felt we were built for it.

Out of the more than 1000 students at my high school there were only about 30 to 50 or so, that were people of color, at that time, so there was an apparent racial tension, and divide.

One day Dave, myself and another friend, Matt, decided to try our hands at armed robbery. Dave had worked at this fast food joint and so claimed he had all the schematics down. On the eve of our plan we walked through the door, pulled our stocking caps down over our faces, and drew our weapons, Matt had one of those big Rambo type knives, with the compass in the butt, and I had a pellet gun that resembled a .357; we had all agreed it would likely be taken for the real thing if I kept waving it. Everything seemed like it was going according to plan, except the part about the manager giving up the money. You see the plan was to enter the restaurant, rustle up the cashiers, and take the manager in the office where the safe, and the nights earnings would be. What we hadn't counted on, was that the floor would be covered in soap and grease, due to it being around closing time and having to be mopped; making it hard to walk, never mind, run on.

Also we didn't consider that the manager would abandon protocol, run and lock the door to the office, and leave the other employees for dead. So we got away with nothing, except that we got away, but you never really get away-not from the highest authority. After continuous battles with my father I ended up back in my old stomping grounds, Utica, N.Y. Things had changed in Utica during my absence, it seemed that cocaine had become popular all over the place, and it just so happened that I knew the guys who knew where to get it.

"NYC to the NYS DOC"

My boy Jay that I had known growing up had a "connect" in Washington Heights. You rarely knew who, and how they got the connections, but if you had one there was money to be made. We'd buy an ounce of cocaine for anywhere from $650 to $900, depending on the prices (illegal markets fluctuate too), and after breaking down those ounces, and packaging them into small baggies we netted anywhere between three to four thousand dollars per ounce, depending on how much shorts (losses) we took.

We'd work until the wee hours of the morning, and sometimes from Thursday night straight through the weekend. That's partly how sniffing cocaine became a habit for me; it was an occupational undertaking-at first. One morning as we were on our way to the Waffle House, for breakfast, I saw some kids from my grade heading to school, I felt so low because even though I was making money, I knew I wasn't headed in the right direction. Spiritually I was in a coma, and my downward spiral just continued from there, but not for long.

On the morning of November 23, 1989, which happened to also be Thanksgiving; I was involved in a shooting. My cousin who shares the same first name as me, but who is slightly older, had come down from Rochester, N.Y., the night before. We had gone out and had a good ole time and then returned to my sister Jerri's apartment where I had been staying. As the party continued back at the apartment the doorbell rung, and someone, who, I don't know, answered the door, and before I knew it, there were a group of unfriendly guys, in the apartment.

You see some of the guys that I ran with back then were getting leaned on (extorted) by some of these very guys now standing in my sister's living room. They had come looking for the other guys, but were just as pleased with finding me. Robert Garrett aka Rakim was one of my guests in the house. We had gotten close over the course of the last couple of months, and he was a part of the crew I hung out with. An altercation erupted, and shortly after, spilled outside onto the porch. Rob was trying to play peacemaker, but I had already armed myself with a .22 caliber target pistol. I stepped off the porch and gave the intruders an ultimatum. When they neglected to leave, I began firing, and kept firing in their direction as they fled, feeling exhilarated to see them running. I don't know exactly where my cousin Marcus was at the time, but I noticed Robert looking at me shaking his head, with his hand on his side as he slowly walked to the sidewalk and lay down on the ground.

My exhilaration turned to panic as I ran to him. I could hear the blood curdling in his throat, but he wasn't talking, his eyes now rolled back, and only part way open. I called for someone to call an ambulance, but once the dispatcher heard there had been a shooting they didn't want to send help without knowing what the status of the shooter was, or without the police present.

So we waited for the police for what seemed like 10 or 15 minutes, someone had beckoned me to give them the gun, as I still had it while I cradled Robert.

I don't even remember actually being arrested, that is being handcuffed, and everything else was a blur. I was in a daze; it was like the worse kind of bad dream that I had put myself into, but could not wake myself out of.

By the time I got to the precinct I overheard a cop saying that two men were being treated in the hospital. Minutes later I heard one of the police say laughingly: "Garrett went down south."

The other man Roger, who happened to be the brother of one of my childhood friends, was still in stable condition with multiple gunshots wounds, but Robert had died of one gunshot wound that had entered into his lung through his back, and basically caused him to drown on dry land. It was a nightmare, and I was praying and begging God for Rob not to be dead. I was charged with the shooting of Roger, but in all the confusion, they charged my cousin Marcus with Robert's death.

I had been back in Utica all of 3 months, and now one of my friends lay dead, and however I look at it- at my hand. I knew I would be going away again, for no telling how long.

After a week or so in the county jail I requested a meeting with the District Attorney in an effort to have my cousin's charge of Manslaughter taken off him and given to me. They scheduled a lie detector test in Syracuse, N.Y., during which I answered all their questions to the best of my recollection, but still my cousin Marcus wasn't exonerated. He ended up being sentenced to 1 to 3 years in state prison, and I received 2 to 6 years. I served most of my sentence there in Oneida County Jail. My cousin was bailed out shortly after our arrest, and till this day I have not seen him in all these years. We've spoken over the phone once or twice, but not face to face.

I could never say I'm sorry enough to Robert Garrett's family. His nephew George and I grew up together. Often times when I would run away from home in Utica, I would go knock on George's window; his room was in the back on the first floor. He'd complain about the hour, and the knocking, but he'd always let me in. I knew Rob's mother, sisters, brothers, nieces and nephews. I often think about the day when I'll have to face his offspring. Throughout the years I've prayed for forgiveness, and tried to move forward, but sometimes the past remains present. I hope, and pray I'll be there to welcome Rob back with the countless millions that the Bible holds out the promise of resurrection to. After my initial arrest, I told my friend Ike that I didn't truly appreciate the gravity of the situation until I saw the look on him and his then girlfriend's, our mutual friend face as they brought me in for arraignment. When I saw their expressions, I knew I was in trouble. The news spread all over town, they even covered it in The New York Times.

Robert, and Roger were both very well-known in Utica, and the county jail was in an uproar when they brought me and my cousin Marcus in. They placed us into P.C. (Protective Custody), and kept us there up until finally I had to write a formal request to be released into general population. The threats were still swirling, but I had much bigger things to worry about.

Jail was like Annsville, except there were bars, and cells, and people smoked cigarettes. I was nervous for the first few days, but I soon found some friendly faces and supporters and was able to settle down a bit; it's human nature to look for the best even in the face of the worst situations. Mainly what we did in the county jail was watch television, play cards, and go to the recreation yard to play ball.

At night we'd go to the law library which was also a social center. Preparation for court wasn't the only thing going on in the law library; jail justice was also handed down from the law library as court was held there as well. Who had a problem, with whom, and for what, and how it needed to be resolved. Once a verdict was handed down it was assigned to be carried out.

I studied the law diligently though and so I spent a considerable amount of time in the law library. Out in the streets crack was all the rage and some of my childhood friends was knee deep in the game. We'd hear reports of who had what car, and what girl. We had sold coke in baggies when I had been out hustling, but now it had become bottles or vials of Crack.

They had color tops, and from what I understand, being I missed that whole colored tops era (Thank God), is that the colors, like they often do, identified the seller- It was like an illegal street form of brand marketing.

The music was about to change too; Groups like SNAP, Soul II Soul, and JJ Fad had come, and now on the way were the likes of Main Source, Das EFX, UMCs, Nas, Big L, Black Moon, Mobb Deep, and Brand Nubian, just to name a few. When I was transferred to G-block, which was the cell block for juveniles, I had plenty of time to listen to the radio, being we were locked in our cells most of the time for one incident or another. It was during those solitary moments that I discovered this band-Pearl Jam. I listened to the song "Jeremy" intently every time it came on the radio, which was all the time. I had been in the county jail for almost 18 months, and I would soon be headed to state prison, where I could be released as early as 6 months from then if I was granted parole upon completing my 2 year sentence.

I took my GED in the county jail and scored the highest on record at the time. It was the first time I had really thought about going back to school. I saw the Parole Board while in reception in Elmira, which is not the norm, because reception is normally where you're processed to be placed in another correctional facility based on your sentence, and classification. Once you go through reception, which involves various screenings and processing, you receive a paper that tells you the name of the parole supervisor that you will eventually report to upon your release. I went to reception at Elmira State Penitentiary which is a maximum security facility. I met guys there who supervisors had not even been born yet, nor their parents for that matter; they were instead given, if I remember correctly, numbers that represented someone who had yet to be born.

I remember hearing that Michael Landon had passed away, and how it made me cry. I guess, because I had grown up watching Little House on the Prairie and Highway to Heaven on NBC, in some way I equated his death with the official death of my innocence.

During recreation we'd go out into the yard there in Elmira, which in comparison to the county jail recreation yard, was huge.

We'd gather around and rhyme as someone beat on the guard dog's house, absent the dog of course. I had heard that Tragedy Khadafi, the Hip Hop pioneer from Queens Bridge was in population there in Elmira, but I'd have to wait some years to meet and eventually record with him in NYC.

I ran into a kid named Steve from my old high school in Greece, N.Y., and the funny thing is, neither of us was really surprised to see the other in prison. When the time came for me to see the parole board, the main board member, a woman, Mrs. B, who was notorious for hitting (handing out more time) people at the parole board, grilled me during my hearing. So much so that I thought for sure I would get "hit" by the board which meant I'd have to serve more than my minimum of 2 years, and up to as many as 2 more years.

When the decision came back in my favor I was overjoyed. I was shipped out to a medium security camp called "Washington," which was still in New York State, outside of Albany. I never understood why some of the prisons In New York State, are named after other states.

Washington was a camp similar to Annsville, but with barbed wire, and armed guards. For every maximum prison, there is often a medium prison in close proximity, usually to transition the guys who are getting short (closer to being released). The maximum prison we were close to was Coxsackie and even though it looked like a camp, these were no Boy Scouts.

I ran into a guy in Washington we called "Marty" who I actually had known by another name during my days at Annsville. Washington was a prison for younger guys so there were a lot of emcees there and we got together and performed regularly, we even wrote a song called the "Four Seasons" which buzzed around the whole camp, and maybe even throughout the prison system I imagine.

I was the "Spring," a kid named Skip from the Bronx was the "Winter," Allah who was from Long Island was the "Summer," and a kid named H-lover who was from Brooklyn was the "Fall". A kid named Joe Black, from parts forgotten, even insisted on being "Leap Year" because the song became so popular.

November 1991 would mark two years for me being locked up, and the month came In with a bang. Earvin Majic Johnson would hold a news conference divulging that he had contracted HIV. The ignorance and fear surrounding the disease was then at an all-time high, and we all felt it was a death sentence for him.

When I was finally released on parole it was to my little sister Tammy's house. Cypress Hill was buzzing in the streets with "How I Could Just Kill a Man," Ruffhouse, 1991. I didn't tell B-Real this when we met on 6th Avenue, some years back, but that song echoed the sentiment on the streets of Utica, and I'm sure other cities as well at that time. I had fostered friendships during my time away with many of the people I had met while locked up; many of them from NYC, Brooklyn to be exact, and more specifically East New York, Brownsville, and Flatbush.

Some of them were even at odds with each other when I came home from prison, and so I walked right into drama. There was still money to be made in the crack game, and that brought a lot of enterprising guys and girls from NYC.

Some came to Utica, and others went to surrounding cities. Some were in multiple cities- so the same group of guys that help decimate a small city in Massachusetts; help decimate Utica and so on.

A lot of the guys I had grown up with had also picked up the drug trade, and while I was locked up, some had made quite a bit of money from it.

So there I was back on the street with no real resources. My parole officer was adamant about me finding a job and or going to school so I opted to sign up at the local community college M.V.C.C.

My mother had gone there and graduated so I figured I'd give it a shot. Like high school I showed an aptitude, but didn't follow through with the work, college just didn't interest me.

I felt like we were just sitting around putting labels on things that I already knew, but just not by those terms. For instance I knew from seeing the evolution of Rap to Hip Hop, to worldwide, that if something was popular in NYC, that it would eventually spread and make its way all over the world. I didn't know to call it "Cultural diffusion" though.

Some of the students took their Pell and TAP grants and invested them in the streets, I guess the Government was in on the drug game on more than one level.

I started making trips to New York again. We were actually down in Washington Heights around the time the riot over the cops supposedly throwing a kid off the roof was happening. I heard they had called the National Guard in. I would have never thought that one day I would call that place home.

On one of those fateful trips to NYC, I missed my connecting transport, and was informed that the next one wouldn't be until first thing in the morning. A woman, a stranger who I had only spoken with briefly, offered to let me stay at her place until the morning, I reluctantly agreed, not knowing anyone else to call. She explained that although she was inviting me to her home it wasn't an invitation to her bed. I was just relieved to be inside someplace and off the street, especially considering I had a couple of ounces of cocaine on me.

As we approached her building which was on 129th Street & Convent Avenue - I recognized the address even though I wasn't really familiar with New York. It was with the same address that Kool Moe Dee had popularized in his song "Wild Wild West," from his the album *How Ya Like Me Now*; Jive Records 1988; and as she opened the door to her apartment she turned and mentioned two things in quick succession to me; (1) she had a boyfriend who lived with her; and (2) He was on Angel dust (PCP).

Oh well, I thought, so much for getting any sleep that night. Her boyfriend as it turned out was cool, but just to make sure he stayed that way I chipped off some powder off the package I had, and gave him some. Between him being up all night, and the mice frolicking in plain sight in the middle of the living room, I couldn't sleep a lick. I had stuffed the package into my jacket which I then used for a pillow and could still smell the potent product even through the plastic as I lay on top of it. I was relieved when daylight came, and so I then made my way back downtown.

I would have told Moe Dee that story when I met him at Irving Plaza in Manhattan, but he didn't seem like he wanted to be bothered, and I understood. It must be really frustrating for many of the Hip Hop pioneers to see so many of the newcomers for whom they've paved the way making the kind of money they never did, and not even really paying homage. So most people who approach these pioneers do it only with accolades, but accolades don't pay the bills. As I walked through the tunnel under Time Square I was so happy to be on my way back to Utica. As I turned the corner in the tunnel I came almost face to face with a cop and his canine. The dog went absolutely ballistic as I walked passed, and I thought it was over.

The Utican Part III

Now I know that sounds reminiscent of that scene in <u>Reservoir Dogs</u> directed by Quentin Tarantino, and also written by him and Roger Avary, Miramax, 1992; the one where Tim Roth's character is relating the "Commode" story, but go figure, my life is like a movie.

I would make it back home to Utica safe yet again but soon after more foolishness would ensue. On another occasion while coming to pick up some more trouble, again in Washington Heights, we were pulled over by the police shortly after buying just over 4 ounces of cocaine. Now just over four ounces of cocaine is serious business; according to the law it's in the same class of felony as say a homicide.

The NYPD hopped out of the van and after taking my boy D's driver's license and registration, they returned to ask me my name, and also to ask the name of the girl sitting in the backseat, who just happened to be my girlfriend at the time.

She answered truthfully, but I gave them a fake name, because even if we weren't traveling with narcotics, I was still on parole and thereby not authorized to leave the city limits of Utica, without prior authorization; of which, I had none. So that alone could and most likely would have sent me back to prison. Mind you we had enough drugs to put us all away for what could amount to 20 parole violations.

When the police had initially pulled us over, D, the driver, almost without thinking threw the brown paper bag in the backseat where my girl was sitting. Just as I turned to yell: "What are you doing?" The cops were already outside of our windows. So after they collected D's license, and registration, and as we were waiting for them to return, we sat their discussing under our breath, what our options were: "I'm going to get out and run," I said; I had out run the police before, but that was back home in Utica, not in New York, where I knew almost nothing of the layout. D Protested, and just then the police returned to our windows. They asked D about his license and some clerical matter that he needed to clear up, and he confirmed that it had been taken care of and that he was awaiting the paperwork.

Then the officer asked the girl in the back seat about an incident that she was involved in while in college at SUNY, which she had also since resolved. When the officer finally got to me he asked: "What does your father do for a living?" The question kind of took me by surprise because they had been spot-on with their questions to D and the girl, but I didn't let it faze me, and so I answered: "Construction;" which was true, at least from what I last remembered. It had been some time since I had been in touch with my father.

Being that I didn't have ID on me, I wondered where he was going with that question. They asked D, the driver what he was doing in that neighborhood, and he told them that we were heading to 125th Street to do some shopping, which was also true. D was familiar with New York because he had family that he visited regularly in Newark while we were growing up in Utica, and would visit NYC as well.

The cop told him: "You must've got lost somehow." D insisted that he wasn't lost and that he knew where he was headed. The cop insisted that he was headed in the wrong direction, and all the while I'm sitting next to D wondering why he was arguing with the cop; especially since they had been pretty subdued up until that point.

They asked us all to step out of the vehicle, and then they patted D, and I down, and searched us. There was no female officer present so when they asked my girl if she had anything on her, she, in a panic lifted up her shirt, while inadvertently, and nervously, exposing herself.

The cops now somewhat frazzled quickly instructed her to put down her shirt and sit back in the car. It helped, I'm sure, that the young woman was of Italian descent, because I don't know if they would've been so panicky over a black girl.

They ordered D and I back in the car as well, and then returned moments later with D's license, and a warning about the neighborhood.

As the police got in the van and drove off, I turned to D, who then had the biggest grin on his face, which soon turned into a laugh. Still upset with him about throwing the bag in the backseat, and then arguing with the police, I questioned him on his reasoning. He said that the only way the cop would have truly believed that he was lost, is if he thought he truly believed and was convinced that he knew where he was going.

I couldn't argue with the logic, and just then we both turned to the girl with the same question: "Where are the drugs?" She reached down into her jeans shorts in the small space between her crotch, and pulls out the bag and we were both in disbelief.

Now would you believe that even after all that, I would continue to go down to New York to pick up drugs, and although I never got arrested for drugs, I would end up violated on parole, not only once, but twice, and then a third time, for associating with known criminals, who were narcotic targets, and in one instance, for dirty urine- I had tested positive for cocaine. In the interim of my release and one of my parole violations, I met a young woman who had just arrived in Utica from NYC. She was Dominican, and gorgeous, and I saw her from a moving car and asked the driver to stop. Then I saw her once again as she was heading back to NYC, while on her way to the train station in Utica. I hopped out once again from inside the car to talk to her, and then finally I saw her walking through the cafeteria at the community college, and so I asked her if I could walk with her? That walk lasted about 10 years, and yielded a son.

***

The next time I would visit New York would be under entirely different circumstances. It was the morning that Kurt Cobain was found dead. Being a Pearl Jam fan I had always thought it treason to get too deep into or publicly celebrate Nirvana's music although I enjoyed it. I know Nirvana fans who feel the same way about Pearl Jam's music. It's like the Yanks versus Red Sox; you can still appreciate the individual players, and uphold the rivalry while celebrating the game. However when a player of the magnitude of Kurt Cobain leaves the game, it's felt throughout the stadiums.

I remember now recently, while on my way to the Blue Note Jazz Club, I tried to approach Courtney Love, over by the basketball courts on West 4th Street. I should probably remember not to do that again.

I remember back on that day in April many moons ago, I had gone on a college trip with my buddy Cliff, but instead of going along with the rest of the students to visit museums, we opted to try to go watch the dress rehearsal of *SNL*. We didn't get into the taping, but we had a good ole time outside in Rockefeller Center, where the show is broadcast from, on NBC.

I remember Kelsey Grammar being the host that night and meeting Norm Macdonald after, he was so cool. I also remember mistaking David Spade for Dana Carvey and him saying some sarcastic remark as he walked away.

At that time David Spade wasn't as popular as Dana Carvey or as popular as he would become. Now that I come to think of it; I guess you could attribute my reason for expecting, and holding *SNL* cast members, to such a high standard of cool-to *SNL* cast members themselves. To the Norm Macdonalds, Finesse Mitchells, Rachel Dratchs, and Colin Quinns, just to mention a few now, and more about a few more later-this spanning from years ago until present day.

I remember how excited we were to just be in New York City, and me, especially in the absence of the fear of being arrested, not for any major crimes at least, we did have open containers of alcohol.

Being that I was down in NYC under the guise of being on a college trip, I was even in the clear with parole. I told myself then I would be living down here in NYC one day, and on some level I must have come to believe it.

The last 2 years prior to the trip had proven to be ones of highs and lows. I had been released from prison for a parole violation, and I also managed to get myself shot, or should I say, grazed, in the head. The bullet split my baseball cap up the middle, and literally pushed my scalp back. I thank Jehovah God that I'm still alive, and have my faculties.

Still, I would leave NYC with the college kids, to return to Utica that night in April, and eventually be violated back to State Prison again. Yes the parole department in Utica had it out for me, but I didn't make it any better on myself. It would usually boil down to my association just like from the beginning.

My parole violation most recent to the college trip surrounded a man we called Noot, who was killed, and the people implicated in the murder were said to be close associates of mine. Which was in part true, I knew one of the guys, but the other, I had just recently met, either way I had nothing at all to do with the killing.

In fact it was the brother of a kid I grew up with, whose younger brother had been the victim in a kidnap-murder case that shook our whole community back in the early 80s. The little boy's name was Johnnie Lee Bell, and Noot his older brother now lay dead.

Their mother if I remember was from Dothan, Alabama, the same place my mother is from. Johnnie's abduction and murder had also stuck with me because I had visited that same store that he was kidnapped from, at also around the same time, on that very same evening. That corner store was one block from where I lived, and his family lived one block down and around the corner from my family.

Now their family was rocked with the death of another son, and it was someone I knew on both ends. The detectives interviewed me and felt I had been uncooperative during the interview. They threatened action against my mother for some unrelated, and pending incident, and then finally told me that not only would I be violated back to state prison, but also that around the time I'd be nearing the completion of my violation, they would have another new case waiting for me, and I believed them, although they hadn't believe me.

The Utica Police Department was rumored to be so corrupt at one time that some neighboring police departments wouldn't even share information with them.

I did end up getting violated again, this time for 18 months, the maximum they could give me at the time. I was sent to a medium correctional prison camp called "Wyoming"; right next door to Attica. Wyoming was no joke, it felt like prison, and it seemed like the skies were always grey when I first arrived there.

I was pretty much a model prisoner, I didn't get involved with the drugs or the gangs, and in fact I started to study the Bible again while inside; some of the brothers from the local congregation of Jehovah's Witnesses organized meetings at the prison, which I would attend.

During one of my violations I had been in a prison camp called "Cayuga," not far from Auburn, both the town and the prison. While on a visit, my boots, cigarettes, and some microwavable Cornish hens were stolen out of my locker, and I didn't act according to the unwritten prison rules which dictated that I stab or cut the thief. Instead I basically let it slide after only a minor skirmish. I didn't want to live by prison rules, because I didn't want to live in prison.

I never reported the person who had stolen the items I just quietly finished my time and went home, while watching him wear my boots almost every day.

I had seen instances of guys losing their release dates right before they were set to be released-mostly due to being charged with a brand new crime, or an old or open case catching up with them.

Plus I was tiring of the whole jail thing, and hoping to get my life on track. So In the camp I just kept my head low, and hit the weights. I hung out with some of the more unassuming guys in the camp, and went on visits every now and then.

On one such visit during my time in the correctional facility, Wyoming, Biz Markie was visiting a fellow inmate and I got to meet and even talk to him; it was one of the highlights of my time in prison, which I know sounds weird, but some of my funniest stories and greatest laughs come from my time in prison.

Even though prison is a tough place, and although we were confined to certain areas, from where we could even, and only sometimes visually see, what we wanted most, right there only inches and feet away from us. We made the best of it-reminds me of another place I know.

When I spoke to Biz Markie I asked him about his album and he told me it was called *All Samples Cleared*, Cold Chillin Warner Bros, 1993. I didn't understand the significance until when I later found out about the complications he experienced due to the sample he used in his song "Alone Again;" Cold Chillin, Warner Bros, 1991.

I saw Biz again recently just a couple of years back at BB Kings in Time Square. It was at the Juice Crew All Stars reunion show, and I was hanging out backstage, as he shuffled back and forth, but he didn't seem like he had time to talk because he was hosting the event that night, and I knew how nerve racking hosting can be, just from my experience in smaller venues.

So I didn't try to jog his memory about our previous meeting, however I did see something interesting that night. Everyone rallied around Biz for the first part of the night, but when Busta Rhymes showed up, the attention shifted to him. I kept waiting to see if another big name artist would come, and displace Busta, but it was not to be.

I wondered, why the shift in the first place? Some would say relevance, but that's just a marketing term. In fact it's because of Biz Markie's relevance that you can even have someone like a Busta Rhymes. I said nothing to Busta that night because I had had an experience with Busta in the past that, at the time, left a bad taste in my mouth; that experience would also inform my mind state, and behavior when I would first meet Kanye West.

Both were misunderstandings, maybe more on my part, but looking back one could appreciate where I was coming from, being an independent artist and all. However at the time I couldn't, and still can't appreciate all the woes and worries of being a major artist.

Sitting there back in prison at that time, who would have ever guessed any of this? It would be nearly a decade and a half before these incidents would even transpire. Kanye West was probably just entering high school at the time; this before his becoming and the arrival of *The College Dropout,* Roc-A-Fella Records 2004.

So I did my time, once again and came home, and then got a job through a temp agency. I ended up working for one of the major Insurance companies doing medical billing and data entry.

There was a group of us who knew each other working there: my boy Nelson, who had been there for a while, and my aforementioned cousin, Michael (Mustafa) Jackson, who I mentioned near the outset of this writing, plus friends, and friends of friends.

I had learned to type in the county jail, on this computer program which mimicked Pac-Man, where in order to move your man so-to-speak, you had to type the individual letters on a string of letters set in the maze, as opposed to just moving a joystick.

That's not all I was doing though, I had also started back with the cocaine, even on my lunch breaks, and without the luxury of the somewhat equalizing effect of alcohol, being that I couldn't drink undetected at work. So I would get noticeably and nervously high.

The OJ Simpson trial had ended, and a: "Not guilty" verdict had been handed down. Plus the Million Man March was slated to occur soon thereafter, so racial and racial-gender tension was at an all-time high. My cousin Mustafa decided to go to the Million Man March, defiantly, not having the time off, and was promptly fired upon his return.

I had become such a mess at work that my manager, a petite blond woman, asked the agency not to reassign me. When I questioned them why, all they said was that she said I made her: "Uncomfortable," yeah I bet.

Although I only had several months to go on parole, and as you may have already guessed, I was violated once again. Goodbye apartment, goodbye girlfriend, and goodbye Utica, I had resolved in my heart not to come back there to live once I was freed.

Let's recap; I was originally sentenced to 2 to 6 years. I did 2 years, returned home, and then went back for 8 months, and then I came home again, and then went back this time for 18 months.

Now I was going away again, and this time it would be to complete my sentence, to max out as they say. By the time my hearings were concluded, and my parole violation decision was rendered I was transferred to a prison called Downstate, with only a little over a week to go on my violation and the completion of my sentence.

Unlike Criminal Procedure Law which operates under the standard of "Reasonable Doubt;" Executive Law, which is the law that governs The Department of Parole, operates under the standard of, "A Preponderance of Evidence." Which means that instead of having to be guilty to the degree that a reasonable person would find you guilty, like under Criminal Procedure Law, you just have to seem more likely to be guilty, than not, under the standard of Executive Law.

The truth is though, being violated those various times probably saved my life, and at the least, my freedom.

So many of the guys I grew up with or knew had got caught up in life sentences or killed while I was away, and it's likely that I would have been right there with them, in either of those places, that are no places to be. Being I had only days to go on my sentence I tried to keep myself poised. Plus I had to formulate my exit strategy. I knew that the cops and robbers would be notified of my imminent return to the streets of Utica, but I had different plans; the threats that the police made were still fresh in my mind.

So on the day of my release I kept quiet all the way to the Poughkeepsie train station. As I sensed that we were getting close to Poughkeepsie I asked the two correctional officers who were escorting me in the van, if they had ever heard of a, "Washington Street?" The driver said that it was near the train station, but when I asked if I could get dropped off there he protested. The other officer in the passenger seat told him that I was all done with my time-maxed out, so could be let off anywhere I wanted.

I was gone, and just like I wanted it, without a trace. I had told no one who didn't already know that 3 of my sisters had moved down to Poughkeepsie shortly after I had first gotten into trouble, and they were now, along with my mother awaiting my arrival, in Poughkeepsie yes, God is good, all the time.

"Power Kingdom"

Like people often times, cities have nicknames; Utica's nickname is, "The Handshake City." Its unofficial nickname was, at least in certain circles, "Little Sin City". When I went to take the lie detector test in an effort to exonerate my cousin, is when I found out about the alleged storied past of the Utica Police Department. Cities, like people, can have a hard time shedding their bad reputations too.

Poughkeepsie's nickname is "Power Kingdom," or at least that is how she is referred to in the streets. Now I wish I could tell you that I hit the ground running in Poughkeepsie, but the truth is I loafed around. In part probably because I had no one of authority to tell me what to do, and so I did nothing except sat on my sister's couch, eating her food, and trying to scrape up a couple of bucks for a 40 ounce of beer with some of my newfound drinking buddies.

After some time my father came to visit us from Europe. He had since re-married and moved back to his new wife's home in Holland, that's right, The Netherlands. He urged me to look for work, In fact while shopping at K-Mart he took the liberty of talking to the manager, there and telling her my story, in my absence, and then coming back to my sister's house, picking me up, and taking me back for an interview, that day.

Needless to say I got the job although he didn't show up and work for me; he had just applied myself for me.

Being that I had just come home from prison, and was in good shape the management at K-Mart must've thought it was cool to pay me the wages of a stockperson, but have me double for loss prevention when shoplifters were caught. Or I should say, they did this on one occasion. While awaiting the arrival of the police I concluded that I didn't want to do crime, or crime prevention for that matter, and I certainly didn't want to make that kind of introduction in a new city so I was out of there.

Shortly thereafter I actually got a job as a personal trainer in a health club, but old ways die hard, and I showed up reeking of alcohol and cigarettes for a Saturday morning session, and was promptly taken off the schedule. So I was in a new town and out of work again.

Now to recap, again and to be fair, it wasn't all crime back in Utica either. I had worked at a Pneumatic power tool company on the assembly line with a bunch of Vietnamese who only listened to Country music all day long. Although I didn't learn Vietnamese, I learned that I did like Country music. That was also around the time I worked packing doughnuts. So I wasn't averse to working, I was averse to being among the working poor.

Nelly, my Dominican girlfriend, had since moved back to New York, and would come up to Poughkeepsie on the Metro North to visit me occasionally, but our relationship had become strained. I had even started being abusive towards her.

I signed up with a temp agency and did an assortment of jobs: document disposal, heavy lifting (literally, before it became a euphemism), plus I did some more stock work-I did what I could.

I had an opportunity to go live with my great uncle on my mother's side in Newark, New Jersey, and so I did, but just a few months later I needed to look for a new place to stay. Older people are more distrustful of technology and people than most, and understandably so seeing that they are the target of many scams perpetrated by both. My eighty-something year old uncle didn't understand the concept of calling cards, and so thought I was racking up a phone bill he would have to pay at the end of the month.

One thing I remember about living on the Southside of Newark is not seeing any white people for miles and miles after business hours, and also the symphony of car alarms that would sound off at night, as cars sped by parked cars.

The main thing I remember about living in Newark was while visiting my then newly ex-girlfriend's aunt, on the Lower East Side of Manhattan, I was told that she, my ex, was headed to the hospital that same day. So I made my way over to the hospital, only to find out that she was pregnant. I hadn't talked with her for a couple of months, and now our first conversation would pertain to parenthood. I told her that I'd be there for her, but inside I was afraid. I had, it seemed nothing to offer a child. So after a month or so, and not having a definite place to stay I went back to Poughkeepsie and after a brief layover in Poughkeepsie; I went back to what I knew.

Utica is one of those places with a magnetism, albeit, a malevolent one much of the time. I always tell folks it's the kind of place that you can stop at to get some gas, and end up starting a family and never leaving. Or like me, go there for just the weekend in the spring, after finding out you're going to be a father for the first time and remaining for almost the whole summer.

The prospect of fatherhood, and the mounting expectations caused me to want to escape, and so I ran. I lived off of the excitement and enthusiasm of those who hadn't seen me in a while. I stayed with my boy Ike, who I had known since the early 80's; it was with Ike that I had first recorded music. He would provide beats from his Casio SK-1, back then, I remember being particularly fond of Bossa nova. After a short stay at Ike's, I then stayed with my boy Thom who was at the time on house arrest, and so welcomed the company.

With no job, no money, I still managed to party almost every day. That's what kind of place Utica was for me; easy to live, easy to die. I learned that having a lackadaisical approach to NYC will render you homeless quick, fast, and in a hurry.

Bob a man I met during my exploits on 6th Avenue, and who had picked up music from me, and even backed me on my R.A. the RUGGED MAN event that I threw at the Bowery Poetry Club; asked me where I saw myself in 5 years. My answer seemed to suggest that I need not think that far ahead, that forecasting that far into the future was not necessary.

Then Bob asked me how long he and I had known one another. It didn't seem that long at all, that is until I realized it had been about 5 years. My, how time flies; maybe in some ways I was still on prison time just satisfied with getting to and through days, weeks, and months, not thinking about the years, and maybe I had allowed being in prison to condition me to not concentrate on the future. To do the time, and not let the time do you as they say.

Before I left Utica I realized that I had no allies in the legitimate world. If I wanted a product or service in the criminal world I knew exactly who to talk to; But if I needed say a cosigner for a loan, or anything of that nature I drew blanks. I had invested heavily in the streets, and in the marketplace of the streets, it's not the bulls or the bear that one worries about- it's the wolves.

I think, in part, that in itself contributes to the high incidence of recidivism in the prison system. The path of least resistance is on every corner. That's not a justification, merely an observation.

So I was in Utica with no direction, no ambition, and no solution, then finally I got a call that the Doctor needed to induce Nelly's labor because of her blood pressure. My son would be born prematurely, and I didn't even have the money for the bus ticket back to New York. Thankfully my boy Nelson bought me a ticket, and I jumped on the next bus heading to New York City.

When we pulled into Albany a girl got on the bus, and walks down the aisle looking for a seat. So as I'm heading to watch my son being born, and with no romantic notions towards her, I thought nothing of it as I offered her the seat next to mine.

We talked and found that we both were headed to New York, both to exciting yet fearful and uncertain prospects. She said that she was heading to NYU from Canada. I told her I would be officially entering the institution of fatherhood. Her name was Ann Marie, and sometime maybe a month or so after my son's birth I stopped by the address she had given me. The dorm was in Union Square, close to where my son's mother lived, so I figured I'd go by and see how she was getting by. I couldn't remember exactly where she said her room was so I asked the doorman, who wasn't much help either. So I left not seeing her again that day, or for years after.

Even up until recently whenever I'd see someone who vaguely resembled her I would ask: "Ann Marie?" Until eventually her semblance became a vague memory itself. Recently, some months ago, I see this woman who kind of resembled what I remembered she may have looked like; and her name just happened to also be Ann Marie. After doing a little digging I also was able to confirm that she is indeed from Canada, but not if it was indeed the Ann Marie I had met back late summer of 1997. I couldn't even ask her to confirm her identity, because the day I saw her, she was at work on T.V.

So I arrived in New York City and made it to Beth Israel Medical Center just in time to see my son being born. I was relieved, and I thanked Jehovah God, for my son, and his mother's safe delivery. When I first looked at my son I forgot all about getting high, and what the past few months had been. I had to become a man, and probably for the first time in my life. I stayed sometime in New York with Nelly's aunt to be closer to her and my son. Then I headed back to Poughkeepsie, I had work to do.

Right next to my son's mother hospital room was a young lady who had also just had a son, her name was Lauryn Hill.

***

While in Poughkeepsie looking through the classifieds, I saw an ad in the paper for employment, offering up to a thousand dollars a week. I called the number, and was scheduled for an interview, and on the day of the interview I got up, put on one of the 3 suits I owned, and went in.

It was at a Ford dealership and low and behold I got the job. I looked decent in a suit, and could articulate well, so I guess they figured they'd give me a shot. The guy who trained me name was Bobby, he reminded me of the actor Yaphet Kotto. Bobby was hilarious; he was one of the best negotiators I had ever seen. People would come in loaded for bear, and big ole Bobby would charm and disarm them into a brand new pickup truck. The turnover in the car business is such that you never really get attached to anyone, but it was hard not to get attached to Bobby.

I remember being late for work one day, and the owner of the dealership, a real stern man with a reputation for being tough, pulling me to the side, and telling me: "If I owe you a buck I pay you a buck, don't cheat me out of a nickel -don't be late."

Not long after that I transferred to the Used Car Annex, which kind of felt like jail again, except that we wore nice suits, and ordered lunch from outside, scratch that, in jail we even at one time ordered food from outside, but that's a whole other story altogether.

Then one day while I was on the phone with Nelly back in New York, she heard me and my manager cursing and screaming at each other and she asked me is: "Everything ok?" I told her that it was just the nature of the business, and she encouraged me to find a different business.

That same manager Matt, who harangued me, would also drop me off in Manhattan on some Saturday nights, being that he lived there, and we had Sundays off. He would then meet me, and pick me up for the ride back into work, early Monday morning.

I never made that advertised thousand dollars a week, in fact the few deals I was involved in, got wrestled away by the older and more hardened, I mean, seasoned salesmen. There was this one guy Rich, who could greet you and insult you in the same breath. The dealership had the makings of an HBO or Showtime series.

When I was finally let go, I didn't even go home, I went right down to the Saturn dealership. I don't know why I chose Saturn out of all the dealerships on the strip, maybe because I was looking for something different, and they advertised as a "Different Kind of Car Company".

I got the job on the spot, but one of the first things I had to learn, was to unlearn a lot of the things I had just picked up from my conniving combative colleagues up the road. Saturn taught me not to sell the car on the basis of how much you could save on the sticker price; in fact there was no haggling when it came to price.

We sold cars by educating the buyer (guest) on the total cost of ownership. Once they understood the relationship between maintenance, parts, insurance, safety, fuel economy, and resale value. The process then became a lot easier for them and for me. I did well at Saturn when I wasn't partying, and when I was partying I still did good enough to be missed in my absence when the month's sales were tallied.

When people came in and asked for the number one salesman they were actually introduced to a woman. Her name happened to be Ann Marie as well, and she may have been from Brooklyn if I remember right; but I was usually the number two salesman or at least in contention, month in and month out. I had a decent job there in Poughkeepsie, and was even able to move out on my own. However in an artistic sense I felt discontented.

I never could really get anything going, or completed artistically in Poughkeepsie, and it was depressing; during the almost four years I spent there I never even recorded one song.

Croton Harmon

I would make the effort to come to New York to visit Nelly at least once or twice a month usually on the Metro North. She would also make the trip to Poughkeepsie as well.

I remember being on the same train as Ana Gasteyer, also of NBC's, *SNL* fame. I watched her once as she amused the other passengers and noted how she expressed herself so animatedly. I didn't have the nerve to approach her back then, at least not in the presence of onlookers; it takes a certain kind of performer to step on stage, any stage with a seasoned professional- so I just sat back and admired her from afar.

Another regular on the Metro North was an actor by the name of Adam LeFevre. He's been in tons of movies, and him and I would talk about the arts, and I got a sense from him that he was just appreciative enough, to just be able to ply his craft. That he had little or no aspirations it seemed to be a household name, and on the ride down we'd talk about music, the Bible and Greek mythology.

I would seek out artist types, movers and shakers, and anyone else who looked or seemed interesting, I met a young woman named Rosalind Brown, also on the train to New York. She was a singer, and actor who happened to also be starring in the play *Footloose*, based on the film directed by Herbert Ross, Paramount Pictures, 1984; alongside Adam.

I asked her if she had ever met Kevin Bacon, not thinking I'd ever meet him myself, and she said yes that he had come by the show once or twice. She arranged tickets for me to go see the show, and so I brought Nelly along.

I enjoyed it, but Nelly seemed like she could take it or leave it. The fact that Nelly was born and then partially raised in the Dominican Republic, I think has informed her more pragmatic approach.

I was just happy to know in Adam, and Rosalind, people who were doing something similar to what I wanted to do. I never wanted a big house or car; I wanted to travel, to sail, and fly.

Let me be clear though, I'm a hard worker-I work hard. People who'd watch me work would ask me in a confirmatory tone: "Working hard?" And were amused but not surprised by my response: "Is there any other way to work?"

During my prepubescent years we'd have congregation picnics at a place called Delta Lake in Rome, New York. I loved the ride there, and back; seeing the sun, and then the sunset through the trees, as the light reflected off the water, and bounced back onto the leaves. My father would play The Best of Nat King Cole, Capitol Records, 1968, in his 8-Track. The song "Those Lazy-Hazy Crazy Days of Summer" would blare through the car speakers, and we'd all sing along. I'd drift off, not to sleep but to some distant recess in my mind, and imagine traveling to faraway places. When the song "Mona Lisa" would come on, my father would belt along beautifully accompanying Mr. Cole, and to me it was pure poetry.

The interesting thing to me is when people ask me about my musical influences, I never once remember mentioning Nat King Cole. I guess when asked that question I either immediately try to align or misalign with the person who is asking, or I just take the likes of Nat King Cole for granted considering them to be a given.

Coming up I'd associate Paul McCartney more quickly with Michael Jackson or Stevie Wonder than I would with John Lennon. It was the 80's, The Beatles had long been broken up, and contemporary Pop music was to me, at its finest.

I also didn't recognize Herbie Hancock as a jazz artist either. To me he was a Hip Hop pioneer. Plus I didn't listen to jazz really, until I was almost 40 years old, and living in NYC. I'm happy it turned out that way, to be able to discover wonderful expressions of art and music at this time is refreshing and invigorating; and music can be such a blessing.

So I'd head back to Poughkeepsie feeling artistically deprived hanging out at local college bars playing pool around students who'd just cast me off as a "townie". I continued to dig a hole in myself, and then tried to refill it with more dirt.

What does addiction, and ambition have in common with celebrity, but that they are all forms of escape; trying synthetically, eagerly, and vicariously to inhabit another life, and become people who you are not, in an attempt at leaving your former world behind.

That same drive that drove both my parents' families in some cases to pack fried chicken in shoe boxes, become migrant workers, and leave the south; Has now driven me to forsake my own hometown for yet another place to call my own.

"The End of the Day"

I've met some of the finest actors of our generation, but I wonder if any of them could ever relate to being in a room with two guys from Brooklyn, both who unbeknownst to either, had weapons trained on each other? The one through his jacket, and the other underneath a table, both ready to squeeze at a drop of a hat, and yet they still managed to have the most cordial of conversations, only I being privy to the fact that that this face to face was just a wrong line uttered away from becoming a face off. What did I do? Not a thing except sat back and watched these gripping performances, silently so as not to disturb the scene, hoping that no lines were fumbled.

Daniel Day Lewis picked up my record early in my hustling days. Even after I had at first confused him with Jeremy Irons, who as my mom would say, favors him. He acted as if he knew and understood that it was an honest mistake.

I remember it like it was yesterday, this man walks by wearing green corduroy pants and a dark velvet jacket, and what made him even more curious to me was that he wore loop earrings.

When I first stopped him his face seemed familiar, and as I tried to put a name to the face, the word "day" kept coming up into my consciousness. I thought maybe, the James Ivory directed, Remains of the Day, Columbia Pictures, 1993, based on the Novel by Kasuo Ishiguro, and so I don't know why I blurted out: "Jeremy Irons!" The man just smiled, handed me some cash, and gracefully accepted my record, but as he walked away, a lady who had saw and heard the whole exchange, said to me scornfully: "That was Daniel Day Lewis." So I ran down 6th Avenue to catch up with him, as he was now almost a block away and once I caught up with him I said simply: "The Last of the Mohicans," (dir. by Michael Mann, Morgan Creek, 1992 and based on the James Fenimore Cooper novel of the same name), and then I just walked away, us both with knowing smiles.

I saw him again a day or two later, and asked him what he was working on. He simply said: "I think I'm gonna go, and do a western." That western he referred to, turned out to be There Will Be Blood, directed by Paul Thomas Anderson, Paramount Vantage, 2007, and loosely based on Upton Sinclair's 1927 novel Oil! Which was by definition, a Western, but not the kind of western I had imagined- it had no spaghetti. Which gave me an insight into his simplistic approach to acting, and after watching the film and taking note of all the unspoken nuances; I remember coming out of the theater and coming to the bemused realization that it was indeed a "Western".

I told Daniel Day Lewis at a later juncture about reading the book The Unbearable Lightness of Being by Milan Kundera, Harper & Row, 1984, after only first seeing just a few seconds of the movie directed by Philip Kaufman, Orion Pictures, 1988, as a teenager while my father flipped through the television channels. I may have been tacky in my recounting of the events as his wife Rebecca Miller, a director (and daughter of Arthur Miller, the famous playwright), herself was standing right next to him; Although I did compliment her on her film, The Private Lives of Pippa Lee, Icon Entertainment International, 2009; based on her novel of the same name. I told DDL that I had decided long ago, when I had read that title in the TV guide, that I would use it for one of my albums, and then I just gave that same said album to him. As he walked away I couldn't tell if he was moved, or mad.

Sometimes while working at the car company Saturn in Poughkeepsie, I had to drive to pick up, or drop off, a purchased or requested vehicle at other dealerships for delivery or inspection hopefully by its new owner. I've traveled as far as Medford, Massachusetts, and Long Island. Once I even delivered a car to a student who was just starting at Fordham University in the Bronx. I never actually met the student though; my instructions were to deliver the car to some address on, or near Sedgwick Avenue in the Bronx, and I remember it being a rainy day, and because of not being familiar with the neighborhood I drove slow trying to gauge if the numbers of the addresses were going up or down. I drove past a group of guys huddled underneath an awning who as I passed watched me intently.

I had peeked at the college brochure and was surprised to read in the middle of a glowing description of the school and campus, the writer of the brochure's admission that, besides the occasional gunshot you wouldn't even know you were In New York. I laughed but at the same time I appreciated the honesty. If that student's parent(s) thought enough to buy them a Saturn, then safety was definitely a concern of theirs, and they would deserve not to be deluded in their expectations.

Sad to admit it, but I ended up partying myself out of my new little apartment back there in Poughkeepsie, and back into my sister's housing development, but this time not with her, but in the adjacent building with this guy Lo.

Lo was a straight-edged guy, meaning he didn't smoke or drink any kind of alcoholic beverages. What I personally appreciated about him was that he never seemed to allow himself to lose his temper, yet he was very opinionated. The combination often led to many arguments with just about anyone who engaged him in a lengthy conversation about anything controversial.

Conversations even with his relatives had often led to heated remarks from his opponents, all the while his cooler head prevailed. Not in the argument necessarily, but overall, stress is heavy on the heart.

Even before the internet explosion Lo was into computers and all kinds of gadgets. I was never really into technology, but we both enjoyed music, and so found a common ground there. One night in a drunken groggy haze I stumbled out of the room I rented from him in his apartment, walked down the hallway, opened up the door to my right, like I had done on so many nights, and urinated.

Only the door on the right wasn't the bathroom, or at least not where it had been the night before. I had over shot the bathroom and walked into the closet that was in the living room adjacent to the television. Lo had company over that night, a girl, but he didn't as much as raise his voice at me, only mentioning it in a slightly disappointed tone the next day.

When the film <u>The Matrix</u> came out, directed by The Wachowski Brothers, Warner Bros, 1999, Lo like so many millions was really excited to go see it. I don't' remember if the reason he wanted to go see it in New York was because he just didn't want to see it in Poughkeepsie or if it wasn't showing there, but never needing much urging to go to NYC I agreed to go along.

After the movie was over we caught a cab, because we knew we had to hurry up to make it back to Grand Central Station before the last train to Poughkeepsie left.

As the taxi pulled up to Grand Central Station, we noticed some kind of gala event going on across the street. There were Mercedes, and Limousines that lined the street, and a Red carpet, and a crowd huddled to catch a peak at the event goers.

So Lo and I decided to check it out, only after first going to get our tickets and confirm the departure time. Once we had our tickets, and as we approached the line of people behind the velvet rope, I saw DMC of Run DMC, walk up and then go inside through the revolving door; and then Mary J Blige, and then, this one and that one. I asked a couple of people who stood by what was going on and finally someone told me that it was the After Diva party that VH-1 was throwing for Whitney Houston.

Just then a woman with a clipboard and earpiece approached and instructs the whole crowd to back up. We comply, but minutes later apparently we were crowding the area again. The woman with the clipboard comes back and this time she is noticeably irritated. She looks in my direction and again says: "I asked you already to move back." Frustrated and feeling singled out I moved back again and resolved that if and when she came back I'd have some choice words for her.

She did indeed come back, and with even more attitude, so when she ordered us back again this time I shot back: "Excuse me, but we're supposed to be on the list." She looked me directly in my face as if trying to discern any hint of deception, and then she said: "Oh yeah, what are your names?"

I had a split second to come up with, not one, but two names. They had to be recognizable names, without being recognizable faces. So I responded: "Dame Dash, and Steve Lucas," both names being fresh in my mind, probably because of hoping to see Jay- Z walk by, and having just recently spotted Mary J Blige. The woman then looks at her clip board, searching through the list of names, and then looks back at me and says: "Sorry you're not on the list;" and then she asked us to move back again.

I started to complain as she walked away only for her to reappear minutes later with her clipboard and even more attitude and then she said: "If you don't move, I'm going to have to call security." I responded matching her indignation: "Call security, because I want to know why I'm not on the list, my people are in there and I wanna know."

She asked me for both names again, and again tells me, after checking, that neither names are on the list. She then shakes her head in frustration and walks briskly back up the stairs and into Cipriani's, and reappears, this time with two big security guards dressed in suits and earpieces as well.

She points in our direction, and says: "Those two guys right there," pointing at Lo and I: "Let them in."

At that moment everything moved in slow motion, as Lo and I made our way up the stairs. The sound of the street and crowd became muffled as if I was underwater.

Being now only feet away from the revolving glass door I could see the dance floor was packed. I didn't rush in though, I turned to wait for Lo, like I should, and would have, if we were indeed invited guests, and accustomed to this sort of thing.

From that moment on we couldn't be Dame Dash and Steve Lucas anymore in order not to be found out inside, we just had to be two guys who belonged in there for what reason was nobody's business. Unless of course them stating first what their business was.

Both in jail and in industry events, people who don't readily recognize you often wonder the same thing-how'd you get in here?

Boy did I play the part, the dance floor was like a movie; Wesley Snipes, Mary J, Treach, Timbaland, Molly Shannon, and Cheri Oteri of, you guessed it, *SNL* fame (the former whom I even related this story to after she picked up a record). Everywhere I looked there was a familiar face.

I even made somewhat of a scene when the venue ran out of Moet, so they ending up sending one of the tuxedoed clad waiters to ask me if another brand of champagne would suffice, and upon tasting it, I agreed that it would.

As the night went on, I kept thinking that at any moment someone would catch on.

Timbaland seemed kind of standoffish when I spoke to him, suspicious even; and I wondered if it had something maybe to do with the lady with the clipboard, and who we told her we were.

I just charged it to my paranoia and or guilt over the ruse. I didn't talk in depth to the many celebrities in attendance that night; I just drank and danced, and flirted with Rachel from BET a bit.

Whitney Houston and Bobby Brown were held up in the back area where there were two lines, one in front of her, and one in back of her, of people waiting to meet and greet her.

She was like royalty, and at intervals Bobby would lift her up, from behind and spin her to the opposite line so as to accommodate those in waiting. I didn't stand in line to meet her that night, it seemed too ostentatious, and plus I was having too much fun, partying on borrowed time, little did I know, in a manner of speaking, she was too.

I was drunk off of champagne, and it wasn't a cumbersome kind of drunkenness either-it felt effervescent. I was walking on air it seemed and so much so that we even missed our train and had to sleep on the ground outside of Grand Central Station. I kid you not when I say that as I drifted off to sleep I could still feel my huge smile, and when I woke up, I was still smiling.

Around that same time my son ended up contracting Meningitis. So I left work in Poughkeepsie, and rushed to New York City, to be by his side at the hospital. There are two forms of the Meningitis infection, bacterial, and viral; the former being the more deadly. I could see his mother trying to be strong, but underneath I could sense her worry. I broke down right there in the hospital room, because once again I felt helpless, and I prayed fervently for him to recover.

The doctor was saying that they had to keep an eye on him. He was so lethargic that I didn't know what to do. I only hoped that Jehovah God would grant me my prayer. After they gave him some fluids through the I.V., he became responsive almost immediately. We were so relieved, and he made a full recovery thanks to Jehovah God, and the staff at the hospital.

I remember on my ride down on the Metro North to see him at the hospital that day I thought; "What if I wasn't able to make it in time?" I headed back to Poughkeepsie with a new resolve to lessen the distance between us.

One of the kids that I grew up with back in Utica, N.Y., named George was then living in the Bronx. George had attended SUNY Albany, but had since relocated to New York.

I had visited George during his time in Albany, and he even arranged for me to meet Jay- Z, at the after party for the "Hard Knock Life tour." A guy named Tone, who I had been told was one of Jay's people, help to organize the event, and so for much of the night I stood in an empty VIP room while the party continued upstairs, awaiting Jay's arrival.

He showed up finally and as I approached him I opened my jacket, to reveal my innocent intentions. His security person asked him if he knew me and he shook his head in the negative, and then shook my hand. I couldn't say much, I was more star-struck than anything.

Dame Dash and DJ Clue were outside by the van that night in Albany, New York, and eager to see what a platinum chain looked like, I asked them if I could get a better look at it? They looked at me like I was nuts, and then back at each other.

Now usually an artist might not even show up at their after-party, Jay-Z not only showed up, but he had agreed to perform, and as he made his way up on the 3rd level of the club, I rushed up another stairway to get a good spot. As he took the stage, the crowd started to surge in on him, and there wasn't enough security, and I seen a look of worriment come over his face as he surveyed the crowds that seemed to almost want to love him to death. Maybe that was the start of me wanting to be Dame Dash instead of Jay-Z. George had since moved to the Bronx, and was looking for work and reading self-help books and encouraging me to move down.

My very first visit ever to New York that I remember was back in 1979. I remember me my dad and his friend Al, driving in my dad's car and a group of bikers riding on big motorcycles probably Harleys; and as they rode passed us, through the small space that had become lanes for them, one of the bikers kicked my dad's station wagon so hard that I wondered to myself: "What's wrong with people here?"

I also remember buying my first piece of vinyl here in NYC. It was a 45 rpm record of Smokey Robinson's *Cruisin*, on Motown Records. It felt good picking it up for my mom, because I had noticed the soothing effect music had on my mother. She would drink and get irate, and even embarrass us all terribly, but if the right song came on it was like a well-timed tranquilizing dart.

One time at my 6th grade graduation, as I was being honored with an award onstage, she stood up, unmistakably drunk, and shouted: "He got it from me, not his stupid [jack] daddy."

I was mortified and to make things worse when I sat down and looked over to my left, one of my fellow classmates, Alonzo was doubled over laughing and pointing in my direction.

He and I have laughed often about it over the years. It's amazing how certain things lose their sting after a while. I used to despise my mother's drinking. I couldn't appreciate back then, that there's a kind of pain that someone could feel, so as to make them want to numb, injure, and humiliate themselves that is, until I got older.

Now I was going to be moving to the big city, with all its craziness and I had to psyche myself out over the course of those next several months, plus I would be living in the Bronx at that.

I remember back in 1986, again with my father, driving through Brooklyn, and a guy walked passed us in the car with a boom box, and all I heard I thought was the sound of a hard drum, a cowbell, and words that sounded like: "Now that's what happening." It would be months before I would finally hear KRS-One's "South Bronx" B-Boy Records 1986, in its entirety, and recognize it from the fraction of it that I had heard there on Fulton Street. That song and songs like it have shaped a whole generation.

***

So after months of self-motivating quotes, and contemplation, I finally made it to New York from Poughkeepsie, and if you've been paying attention, then you know where the story goes from here: Saturn-to-restaurants-to-the-streets-of-New-York; plus a whole lot of foolishness in between. The first major actor to pick up my record was Matthew Modine.

He walked by one afternoon, and if I'm not mistaken it may have been the same afternoon that I got a copy to Gwyneth Paltrow, despite her handlers trying to dissuade me. I must say that Gwyneth made it her business to come and say hello to me, after she emerged from the store, with her daughter Apple in her arms- lovely.

Matthew had refused my initial offer some days before, but when I saw him again, this time with an attractive woman at his side. I beckoned to him again to: "Check out my record" and as he kept walking I shouted: "I think it says something about the duality of man, sir;" which may not be his exact quote from the movie <u>Full Metal Jacket</u> directed by Stanley Kubrick, and written by Mr. Kubrick, and Michael Herr, Warner Brothers, 1987. Based on Gustav Hasford's 1979 novel entitled, The Short-Timers; but it was close enough that he, I should say she, his wife got the point. I could see that, as he was trying to make sense of what I had said, the woman whom I would come to know as his wife Cari making it clear to him.

He then spun around and came back and picked up my album, and since then every time I've seen him and her both, they've been nothing but supportive.

When I gave him my second album he asked me what it was about, and I told him, in one word: "Hypocrisy." I knew even then that I would have to stop pushing that kind of material in the streets or anywhere for that matter.

So last Spring I stopped selling music on the streets after experiencing a really bad skin infection. I lost my room uptown and had to move to Yonkers, and then to Ellenville, N.Y., not far from the correctional facility I had been released from, completely off of parole supervision 17 years ago. After Ellenville I moved to Fort Lee, New Jersey, with my pal Ben and then to Queens.

After a long stint of boarding I had to surrender to the tide. I mean one can only ride the wave for so long before being a washed onshore. Even if like me, you've only been bed and couch-surfing, there comes a time where any and everything subject to time and tide, comes to an end.

So I conceded finally, like a candidate after a hard fought, but lost battle, and went and signed into a homeless shelter. I sobbed as I sat there and waited to be processed (people and food are naturally better un-processed).

Not that I hadn't felt shame before, but because I thought it all a thing of the past. A man that is bound before he is done away with doesn't only lament his eventuality, but his ineffectiveness. That was day one- I thanked Jehovah God, and begged for his spirit to guide and protect me, and then I slept, and slept well.

 Day two: I thanked Him for waking me up and for the rebuilding that has already begun now after my breakdown. I went and grabbed some of my things from my old place to bring to my new place, and felt a freedom and fire that not even the cold rain could deny or damper. I returned somewhat triumphant back to the shelter and was tickled all day by the way the caseworkers referred to us all as "clients" and shuffled many papers to be signed, that combined seemed, ironically-at least to this homeless guy, like we were buying houses.

While living back at Richie's place in Harlem years back, I had finally read The Autobiography of Malcom X, by Alex Haley, Grove Press

1965. During the time I was reading it I could envision some of the scenes and the sounds in the book as I walked the streets of Harlem.

Something happened to me in New York. The stain becomes all the more visible under the black light found outside of the big bright city. I remember the thing I most liked and despised about people from the "City" who had come to Utica, for one reason or another was their sheer contempt for everything not NYC. Complaining about the lack of places to go and things to see- name dropping and sharing between them, what sounded to we Uticans, like inside an inside joke.

When the towers fell on 9/11 people filed into the streets in Time Square to watch it all on the big monitors, very much like what's been depicted in some movies surrounding cataclysmic events. Even in horror, here in New York is where art and life sometimes become indistinguishable. New York as a whole has been like that for me, it is both where the cream rises and where what has been set astir settles. I've found that if a stranger is just a friend that you haven't met yet- then a celebrity is just a stranger- you think you know.

Some months ago, a man entered passed me as I sat on the A train. As he rushed passed I could feel and smell a rush of funk, the kind of horrid stench you smell, especially on the NYC subway that makes you feel somewhat trapped. It waned after a short time, but as the doors reopened and closed it would return again with the shuffle of passengers.

The malodorous man spoke angrily and through his teeth, as if his jaw had been broken. A group of young women had entered the train dressed in what look liked chef's uniforms, all holding bouquets of flowers, giggling like girls do. The angry man then looks across to the younger man with whom he had first entered the train car. He signals with his hands and through short but gruff grunts asked for an ink pen. The younger man obliges and announces to the giggling girls condescendingly, that they knew nothing of the man's situation as if to justify his own sympathy.

The angry man continued struggling to get the words not out of his throat or diaphragm, but through his teeth: "Tony Atlas," the angry man seems to be saying, but the younger man doesn't recognize the name. Apparently he and the angry man had resumed the conversation they were having on the platform awaiting the train. In his frustration the angry man repeats: "Tony Atlas," the younger man in his ignorance misses the import and I realized at that moment that the angry man is maybe trying to give the younger man, Tony Atlas' contact information.

The subject they had been discussing was obviously, weight training, and I also think I recognize who the angry man is. He is a boxer who at one time was pretty popular, or I should say well-known, seeing that they are not one in the same.

It seemed now however that life had beaten the angry man down, and so aware of his own wretchedness, maybe he sought now to salvage any sense of his past self, and self-respect by passing on something of value to the younger man. In part I imagine because he wanted to and in part because the younger man had availed himself of it by his humane treatment of the angry man.

As the train neared his stop and having had his cryptic offer refused by the younger man, he just stood there shaking his head as if to say to us all: "If only you knew who I once was- once upon a time." It then dawned on me at that moment that, "Once upon a time" is how fairytales both begin and end.

Famous: Last Words

Over the years I have had the opportunity to not only work with some incredibly talented people here in New York City, and abroad, but with some of the very people that inspired me to make the trek even within my own family, my sister Mrs. Jerri Lorell, and her daughter my niece Jeneva, who taught herself to play the piano, and now even to engineer music, and can be seen drawing and painting in between vocal takes. I feel I pale as an artist when I'm around her. I even had the opportunity to write and record music with my son. Jehovah God has indeed blessed my family very much.

I have to give a shout out to some of my creative comrades in the arts by name: Conrad, Wicz, Brotha-Wex, Frank Lacy, Scram Jones, Eric "Dayta" Lee, Stan, Amore, DJ Lil Ray, John Malozzi, Remy Athacou, DJ Mocha, Lucie Novoveska, Dave Gargani, Michael Ian Farrel, DJ Ready Cee, DJ Mixx, Agallah, DJ Cool Hand Luke, John and Rocco Malozzi, Lucas Machowski, Beef, Game Records, Doug and Dave, Valerie Kuehne, Wonder Twinz, AV8, Dave Hahn, Sway, Truly Odd, and Pacool. All are amazing talents with good eyes and ears to match- with whom I was able to achieve many of my artistic milestones.

In fact you can assume that everyone I mentioned in this writing, in a creative sense is talented. Some people are attracted to the big baller types; I'm drawn to big balls of talent. Be sure to throw a little of those accolades your way as well, because we've all been endowed with gifts.

I've cleaned up my act as far as the sex, drugs, and rock & roll goes, and the only person I seek to impersonate or I should say, imitate now is Jesus Christ. It's a constant struggle, but thanks to God, and with his continued help, I'll come off "completely victorious."

If you haven't already surmised this, my brushes with celebrities, and fame were topical at best. The real substance of these accounts lay with the people, whom you have probably never heard of.

In the early fall of 2013 during the time I was finishing much of the writing on this piece, and as I happened to be standing where I once stood often, there in front of Life Thyme, on 6th Avenue. The singer Usher walked up, and into the store followed closely by a corn fed security type. Without thinking I uttered his name only to be Ssshhhed by the aforementioned security.

I asked the gentleman, who resembled Tom Welling on steroids, what he was: "Talking about?" In a slightly militant tone mingled with a little Arnold from *Different Strokes*.

As I reminded him of my freedom of speech, I then caught myself, because I realized that a situation like that could easily turn to pure pandemonium for the singer, and so I relented. Plus since I had no music to offer him, I realized that I really had no business talking to him anyway.

I had stopped pushing my CDs on the street and started revamping my lyrics and songs, because for a long time I knew that I couldn't publish both the Good News (Gospel), and bad news. That truth became even more apparent after a woman accompanied by her friend had picked up my record months before, just down the street from the Blue Note.

We had a small chat in the moments afterward, and then I tried to share a Scriptural thought with her. She quickly pointed down to the cover of my disc at the explicit label, and I got the message. I couldn't reconcile both. Like the Scripture says: "A spring does not cause the fresh water, and the bitter water to bubble out of the same opening, does it?" I had to change one, and since the Word of God cannot be changed, it had to be my words.

The last celebrity, who picked up my record, before I decided to hang it up, and change up my swing, was Robin Thicke. It occurred one afternoon when I was standing on 6th Avenue near 8th Street.

A black SUV pulls up with the back windows rolled down, and gets caught at the light right in front of me. I could see that it was Robin Thicke seated in the back, and so I asked his permission to approach the vehicle. He said: "Sure," and so I went over and we made it happen right there in the span of traffic light. I thanked him and offered my songwriting abilities, and then he was off.

I didn't try again to engage Usher when he re-emerged from the store that afternoon. I had learned my lesson from Slick Rick. One day when he was slumped up against this silver Range Rover smoking a cigarette on 8th Street, I called out to him: "Slick?" and he responded: "No."

Now of course I knew it was Slick Rick, but what I had ignored was that he wasn't denying his identity, he just didn't want to be bothered. I can't say I blame him either, I feel the same way sometimes, and I'm not even famous- except maybe in certain small circles of famous people. I imagine that even famous people don't want to be famous all the time.

As Usher walked passed me, a woman came out of the building next door that houses both a body work and tarot card establishment; she asked the singer if he'd take a picture with her young son. He obliged, and in one motion leaned over in the little boy's direction, slid off his red Beats by Dre headphones, and held up the peace sign for the picture.

I smiled for the same reason that he agreed to do it. I knew it had made the little boy, and his mother's day. If only for a moment they were able to step into his dimension, or dementia, I forget, just kidding. Maybe it's the convergence of fantasy with reality each fed by the other that draws them and us together.

I checked my phone right after the singer disappeared, and saw a post that read: "Wait, success is just around the corner." Just then, and in quick succession, two fellow artists, Red Clay, and Henry Quester walked by and greeted me. Then I heard a voice call out from down the block: "Marvalous;" it was Metal Mike, another neo-nomad in the streets of NYC. Mike and I spoke briefly about Tragedy Khadafi, the legendary Queensbridge rapper, who we are both acquainted with. I told Mike that I hadn't heard from Trag in a minute, and asked him if he had heard anything. He responded that he had not too long ago spoken to Capone, one of Trag's protégés, and a rapper in his own right, but he had not heard anything recently from the man himself. I showed him the photo that I'm hoping will be the front cover of what you now hold in your hand.

It's of me, my back to the camera, walking down 6th Avenue toward West 4th Street at night, flanked by images of people, some more obscured than others. I had just picked up the file earlier that day from Obarh the photographer (a book unto himself). It had been over a year since I had asked Obarh to snap the photo for me. I told him that it would be used for an upcoming project of mine, and then told him to snap the photo at will, and just left it at that. I asked Mike what he thought of the picture, not telling him anything further. He paused, and as he did, I could sense he wanted to rush off as usual. After pausing for a brief moment of contemplation, he picked up his pace and as he hurried away he said: "I like it, especially the yellow tint." Later that night, my son would also state his approval of the photo, as well. As I stood there, admiring the yellow tint myself, and considering the success that lay just around the corner, I could only think of one word-sublime.

Finally I'd like to give a special shout out to some of the people and places whose names and instances I didn't in whole or in part, include in this writing. A few of you didn't pick up music from me, and yet you still made a contribution. Thank you: PBS, Charlie Rose, and the Public Library System (Ellenville, Manhattan, Queens, Bronx, and Brooklyn), and thank you Google, Wikipedia, and IMDb. All Scriptures cited, unless otherwise noted, were taken from the New World Translation of the Holy Scriptures published by Watchtower Bible and Tract Society of New York, INC, Printing copyright 2013.

Jerry Seinfeld got a record from me outside the movie theater on 13th & Broadway after a movie date with his wife. This before Larry David took one, but after, I spoke with Michael Richards honestly and openly about racial epithets, once he had picked up a record of course. Michael Rapaport gave me the <u>True Romance</u> shirt right off his back while filming his film, <u>Beats Rhyme & Life: The Travels of A Tribe Called Quest</u>, documentary, Quest Sony Pictures Classic, 2011, at Fat Beats. He was actually in the film <u>True Romance</u>, directed by Tony Scott, and written by Quentin Tarantino, Warner Bros, 1993. Thanks Louis C.K., Artie Lang, Michael Wolfe, Jackie "The Joke Man" Martling, Donovan, Ray Romano, and Bebe Neuwirth. Holly Hunter supported me, and so did Jeremy Sisto, and Lili Taylor both, on the same day. Thank you Uma Thurman for your perfectly timed support, and rejection of the French girl's request to take a picture, especially after she had just been rude in rejecting my record, just moments before you walked up and bought it. Bret Ratner picked up a record from me on Broadway, as did Gavin Rossdale & his wife Gwen Stefani (skin like a porcelain doll). I can't forget Charlize Theron (wow), Ace Frehley, Rosario Dawson, Eve Ensler, Mark Margolis, F. Murray Abraham, Amos Lee, Tim Reynolds & Fluffy, Jennifer Esposito, Robert Townsend, Ellen Barkin (and George), Kool Keith, , Chris Tucker, John Leguizamo, Fairuza Balk, Steve Earle, Dr. John, Mr. Tommy Hilfiger, Gaultier, Wendy Parr, Liev Schreiber, and Joaquin Phoenix (thank you for keeping it real). Thank you mister Vin Diesel and I understand how you got distracted, (Luke dancer). I got a record to just about the whole cast of *The Wire*, even recorded a song with Idris (Big Dris) Elba. Also got music to a handful of the cast from *The Sopranos*, (my boy Rocco was in the the episode set in Italy), Oh shout out to Steve Van Zandt, the best onscreen Consigliere since Robert Duvall's Tom Hagen (Based on <u>The Godfather</u>, written by Mario Puzo, and directed by the aforementioned Francis Ford Coppola, Paramount Pictures, 1972) and for supporting the Boss with your guitar and voice onstage; and thank You Sean Lennon and Charlotte Kemp Muhl, and can't forget Grouplove, and Brandon Boyd.

I even started chipping away at the cast of *Entourage*, Rhys Coiro and Emmanuel Chiriqi, Kevin Connolly, Doug Elin, and shouts to Carla Cugino as well, I see you. Also *Boardwalk Empire*, the aforementioned Steve Buscemi, Michael Shannon, Michael K. Williams, and Paz De la Huerta (I should have a deal with HBO). I hit Zab Judah with an album; hit being a colloquialism meaning I gave him a record. Shannon Briggs thanks for even knowing about Utica. Jason Lee, Alec Baldwin, Andre Royo, Roger Guenveur Smith, Chris Rock , Max Weinberg, Jill Hennesy, Mark Ronson, Alexander (it's a family affair), and Mick Jones. Thank you Bill Cosby, Harry Belafonte, Raven Simone, Giancarlo Esposito, Jeff Ross (you really are famous), John Sally, Nelly Furtado (?) , The Rascals, Ryan Adams, The Artic Monkeys, Marcus Mumford, Josh Lucas, Michele Monaghan, Guy Pearce, Kristen Johnston, Vincent D'onofrio, Sebastian Bach (Skid Row), Darryl Jenifer & HR (Bad Brains) Jessie L. Martin, Will Smith (un huh) , Paul Banks and Sam Fogarino (Interpol), Milo (RA RA Riot), Travie McCoy (from outside of Rochester to Utica) Michael Hoffman, Jean Reno, Doug Limon, Craig Bierko, Jessica Lange, Sam Shepard, Ricky Powell, The Beastie Boys, Chris Robison (The Black Crowes), Lyor Cohen, Mos Def (and his mom), Catherine Keener, Moby, Adrien Brody, John Legend, Whitney Cummings, Jeaneane Garofalo, Topher Grace, Julianne Moore, Kirstin Dunst, Joy Bryant, Bill Pullman, Erykah Badu, Gerard Butler, John Singleton, Elizabeth Berkley, Sandra Bernhard, Erika Kristensen, Alana de la Garza, Billy Crudup, Zachary Quinto, Nicole Beharie, Noah Emmerich, Ethan Hawke, Gary Winick, Yancy Butler, Michael Stipe, Mr. Jackson (Jack), Dr. Miller, Elle Varner, and Will Patton who has probably starred alongside many of the above mentioned I can't forget Kurt Loder, J Mascis, Matisyahu, Jon B, Lupe Fiasco, Killer Mike, Beck Lee, Mike Ladd, Jesse L. Martin, Garrison Keillor, Bun B, Good Charlotte, Lenox Lewis, Thomas Hart Shelby, Bob Holman, Hassan Johnson, Isiah Whitlock Jr., Glynn Turman, and Just-Ice. These are just some of the people who I happened to recognize.

A very special thanks also and especially to the multitudes who supported me, all whose names I can't list here, but I may make a space for you to include your names and stories online if you so desire. I'm also interested in those I came across whose work is more recognizable than their faces. I am in fact one of those people myself. I really want to thank Tejas Desai for his insight, and thank the whole Smashwords team: (Marcus V, Raylene, Aaron, and Mark Coker) who helped make this dream of mine, of becoming a writer - a reality. This is for all my fellow hustlers, who hustled before it counted, or could be counted - or who could count – on the internet.

Epilogue

On the eve of Drake hosting *SNL* for the first time I decided I take my son and wait outside to see if we could catch a glimpse of the rapper. My son being such a huge fan of Drake's, and me successfully engaging Pearl Jam in the same place, and fashion several years earlier, I figured, it would be worth a shot. My son seemed ambivalent about the idea. In part, doubting the feasibility of the whole thing; and I could sense that he didn't want to be set up for disappointment. So we get to Rockefeller Center, and after ascertaining that Drake had already gone inside, and also after checking to see if there was any way possible to get tickets outside- maybe somebody had an extra, because somebody didn't show possibly. This too proved fruitless-so we waited. I brought my son to the exact area that I had waited and was greeted by Pearl Jam as they approached the adjacent adjoining garage by the studio back in 06'. I had actually talked to the whole band that day, and talked so fast and so nervously excited that I don't think any of them got a word in edgewise. Now I was hoping to make something special happen for my son. So we waited, and although this was no official concert, I learned that at concerts especially, just like with most things, something special can happen just by showing up. So we stood around for quite some time before the show started, and through its duration, and even as some of the cast left afterwards. All the while I paid close attention to my son as he was almost now aggravated with anticipation. I recalled that part of the reason I had been successful at getting Pearl Jam's attention was because I had my "Alive" Stickman shirt on that I had purchased while in Amsterdam. I at one time even had the original shirt with the original track listing too. So I was pretty hard to miss, plus being a chubby black guy didn't hurt either. So I told my son we needed a sign. There were twenty or so other die- hard fans gathered with us, and teams canvassing the area. I knew from prior experience though that where we were standing was a good spot. So I took the composition notebook out my bag and with a Sharpie scrawled the words "Take Care;" which at that time was the title of Drake's highly anticipated album on Cash Money Records, 2011. So now we had a good spot and even a make- shift sign. I could now see my son was starting to feel good about our chances. After some time the SUVs that had started coming out of the garage, were becoming few and far between. So now we all clamored together, me, my son, a couple of young guys, and a gaggle of young girls, yet I felt neither out of place nor embarrassed.

I saw Andy Samberg being driven out in an SUV, along with other passengers; one if maybe I began to wonder, could be Joanna Newsome? I digress. Moments later a black Cadillac Escalade pulls out slow, with the back windows down, and we could clearly see Drake. Pandemonium ensues, my son and I wave our sign, young girls scream, horns blow, and the Escalade then diverged into the street, picked up speed and headed eastward.

Just then a young man out of the crowd, who kind of resembled one of the young actors from the CW's, *Everybody Hates Chris* show, breaks out in a full speed dash behind the Escalade. Before our disappointment can even set in, we started cheering on this young man. He runs for what has to be close to a hundred yards and as I move toward the middle of the street to get a better view. I can see that the Escalade has stopped, and the boy is now on the side of the vehicle and appears to be talking to someone inside. I wait as the young man returns, and commend him for his determination. Then I asked him: "Well what did he say?" He told me that Drake said to him: "Now that was impressive."

As I looked over at my son I could see his disappointment, and so later that night I broke down and cried. Not because my son didn't meet Drake, but more because he didn't meet the prospect of meeting Drake with the same determination as the other kid. It wasn't about the meeting as much, for me, as it was about the determination. Earlier that night, while we were scoping out tickets holders, I saw a handful of children of privilege, who had the elusive tickets. I knew that I was not in any position to get my son in to see Drake with just a phone call, and I also knew that what we lacked in connection could be made up for in conviction. That young man who chased down the SUV didn't foresee that particular scenario. He just decided that no matter what, he would accomplish what he set out to do. My son, maybe because of his fear of disappointment, unwittingly resigned himself to it. I realized that although I could get him in position, and even get him some tools to aid him. He'd have to have his own determination. Not only in regards to music, but everything.

While pushing my music on the streets, I had to overcome the same kind of thinking in order to put myself out there. Many now do it via the internet, I call them 64-bit hustlers; but being out there on the frontlines connecting with people gave me the wherewithal, and presence of mind that is actual - not virtual, swimming upstream through schools of NOs, just to get to the yes. Sometimes the things we want are right over there- just on the other side of no.

*"The replication of small efforts will accomplish
much more than the occasional use of great talent."*

-Charles H. Spurgeon.

About the Author

Marcus Xavier Taylor was born on September 18, 1971 in Utica, New York. However his arrival to New York City was a gradual one, a sort of geographical putting of his big toe in the water. First immediately after being released from the Downstate Correctional Facility, he relocated to Poughkeepsie, N.Y., where he spent much of his time holding down various odd jobs, and trying to match wits, and pool sticks with the college kids. Then after a short stay in Newark, New Jersey, and a brief return to Utica, N.Y., he finally made his way down to NYC, at around the turn of the century. There he continued for a short while as a car salesman in the Bronx, all the while never abandoning his dream of being a Hip-Hop artist.

After his arrival to New York, and subsequent firing, he then not unlike many, became a waiter; Moving from one waiter gig to another, until finally his failing health, mounting bills, and a desire for a better life for his son, prompted him to seek out trailblazers, and commence to set fire. First through hand to hand street marketing of his own music on the streets of New York City and abroad, and then founding and producing a show (Fire Your Boss presents..., Village Voice pick 2007), at the Bowery Poetry Club. This in turn opened up doors, both literal and metaphorical. All the while, battling addiction, eviction, and ambivalence; hoping and praying to find his way back onto the path of righteousness.

Connect with Me:

Website: http://www.MARVXLOUS.com

Twitter: Ihopeyoudiy

Blog: http://fireyourbosspresents.tumblr.com

Made in the USA
Middletown, DE
13 November 2023

42469976R00097